Thomas Michell

Christian Manhood

Memorials of a Noble Life

Thomas Michell

Christian Manhood
Memorials of a Noble Life

ISBN/EAN: 9783337373115

Printed in Europe, USA, Canada, Australia, Japan

Cover: Foto ©Lupo / pixelio.de

More available books at **www.hansebooks.com**

CHRISTIAN MANHOOD

OR,

MEMORIALS OF A NOBLE LIFE,

BEING

BIOGRAPHICAL SKETCHES

OF THE

REV. R. S. BLACKBURN,

MISSIONARY TO FERNANDO PO, WEST AFRICA.

BY

THOMAS MITCHELL.

"Not seeking mine own profit, but the *profit* of many, that they may be saved."—*Paul.*

LONDON:
JOHN DICKENSON, SUTTON ST., COMMERCIAL ROAD, E.;
BEMROSE & SONS, 10, PATERNOSTER BUILDINGS;
AND DERBY

PREFACE.

 PREFACE to a book, like a porch to a building, should, with the least delay, introduce the reader to the literary edifice. These pages have been written at the request of the relatives of the deceased, and as " Memorials of a Noble Life," it is hoped the perusal of them will stimulate others to the pursuit of things that are excellent.

A good life, fairly put on record, acts like an inspiration to others. It shows what man can *be*, and what man can *do* at his best. It exhibits what life is capable of being made. "The good life," says George Herbert, "is never out of season."

A celebrated Essayist affirmed that " Biography is either ignorant or partial : ignorant, if written by a stranger ; partial, if written by a friend." If friendship be a disqualification for our task, we must plead guilty to it. A close intimacy in ministerial work, for over three years, gave us an insight into, and a high appreciation of Mr. Blackburn's Christian character, awakened the conviction that a multiplication of such men in the ministry would be an incalculable boon to the church, and resulted in sincere friendship between us.

It has been the writer's earnest aim to give a natural and straightforward account of a good life, containing, indeed, not much of the marvellous, but marked by earnest, plodding, persistent toil for the welfare of men.

A melancholy interest gathers around the name of the subject of these pages, from the fact that he was the *first* Primitive Methodist Missionary to die in a heathen land. Hitherto, we have happily enjoyed an immunity from such losses, and, though with enfeebled health, our brethren have yet been permitted to return home to recruit. Now, we are called upon to share with other Missionary Societies, this trial and honour also, that our agents, after a brief period of devoted toil, sometimes die at their post.

My thanks are due, and are hereby cordially tendered, to the numerous friends, whose contributions appear in this volume.

Should the circulation of this work prove remunerative, the claims of the African Mission Fund will not be forgotten.

That these "Memorials" may be used by the Master as some contribution to the extension of His kingdom, and especially to the spiritual and material welfare of the tribes on the African continent, is the Author's earnest prayer.

T. M.

81, *Rectory Road, Burnley.*

CONTENTS.

CHAPTER I.
PROMISING BEGINNINGS—

SECTION I.—BIRTHPLACE AND BOYHOOD ... 1
SECTION II.—CONVERSION ... 5
SECTION III.—CONSECRATION ... 14

CHAPTER II.
CHOSEN SPHERE ... 29

CHAPTER III
FAITHFUL TOIL—

SECTION I.—BINGLEY ... 51
SECTION II.—FERNANDO PO ... 93

CHAPTER IV.
EARLY REST ... 145

CHAPTER V.
FRAGRANT MEMORIES—

SECTION I.—ESTIMATE OF CHARACTER AND MINISTRY ... 170
SECTION II.—TESTIMONIES TO WORTH AND SERVICE ... 179
SECTION III.—LETTERS OF CONDOLENCE ... 195

MEMOIR OF REV R. S. BLACKBURN.

CHAPTER I.

Promising Beginnings.

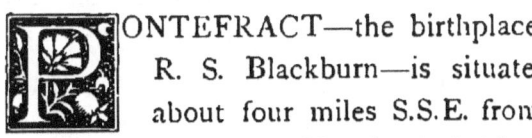

"From a child thou hast known the Holy Scriptures, which are able to make thee wise unto salvation through faith which is in Christ Jesus."—2 *Tim.* iii. 15.

"Let your objects be high and holy, and then the High and Holy One will give you strength and grace to attain them."—*Anon.*

SECTION I.—BIRTHPLACE AND BOYHOOD.

PONTEFRACT—the birthplace of the late Rev. R. S. Blackburn—is situate on an eminence about four miles S.S.E. from the confluence of the rivers Aire and Calder in Yorkshire. It is a well-built town, with spacious streets, Town Hall, Market Hall, Grammar School, and the ruins of an ancient Castle. Architecturally, these ruins are not important, but the historical associations are numerous and interesting. The castle was founded soon after the Conquest (1066), and held in 1310, by Albert de Lacey, when it passed into the hands of Thomas Plantagenet, Earl of Lancaster, and nephew of Edward I., who resided, and was beheaded there, in 1322. There also John of Gaunt lived; and in his early youth Henry of Bolingbroke. There, too, came also, as a prisoner, the unfortunate Richard II., and within its walls was murdered. The Dukes of Bourbon and Orleans, taken prisoners at Agincourt in 1415, were sent to Pontefract Castle, where they remained for many years, with an illustrious prisoner who afterwards joined them—James I., the young King of Scotland. There also Earl Rivers and his chief associates—murdered by Richard III. in 1483—were added to the sanguinary catalogue of noble sufferers. Anciently, it was a "high and stately, famous and princely, impregnable castle and citadel, which for situation, strength, and largeness might compare with any in this kingdom." It was thrice besieged during the civil war, and dismantled by order of the Parliament.

Below the ruins of Pontefract Castle stands the old church of All Saints, itself also, almost a ruin. Its walls fell before the cannon of the Parliamentary Generals after a resistance of nearly three years, in part of which both Cromwell and Fairfax were present. A Priory and Convent, then annexed to it, were totally destroyed. In 1837 the central tower and transept were repaired and fitted for Divine worship; and in 1860 a considerable sum was spent in restoring the same, and strengthening and supporting the ruins. The church appears to have been early decorated with perpendicular insertions. The tower contains a double geometrical staircase, worthy of notice. A singular inscription on a tomb in the churchyard attracts the attention of those curious in such matters. It runs as follows:—

"Eye findeth, heart chooseth;
Love bindeth, death looseth:"

the four nouns being represented by symbols. The Wesleyans, Primitive Methodists, Independents, and the

Roman Catholics, are all well represented by chapels and schools.

The soil around Pontefract is extremely fertile. Liquorice is largely grown in the neighbourhood, and made into "Pomfret Cakes." The plant is very graceful, and does not come to perfection till the third year. The population in 1871 was 11,653, and it returns two members to Parliament. Malting is carried on extensively in the locality; and coal mining, breweries, tanneries, machinery, and corn mills supply the inhabitants with occupation.*

Here Richard Stead Blackburn was born, on November 5th, 1850. His father, whose name he bore, occupies a respectable position as a tradesman in that ancient borough, carrying on an extensive business as an ironmonger and general furnisher. His mother, Harriet by name, died after a prolonged affliction, while he was still a youth. Richard's early years seem to furnish few incidents calling for special remark. His boyhood and youth were of such a character as is usual in the station in life in which he moved; and not many events partaking of the marvellous or heroic entered into his experience at this period of his career.

He received the customary education of a youth intended for business pursuits; and exhibited during his school-days exemplary diligence in his studies, and commendable behaviour in general. His father testifies, "I never had a complaint from school as to his behaviour; and one of his teachers affirms that he never had to punish him, once, for misconduct."

---

* "Yorkshire: Past and Present." Baines.

He shared the inestimable advantages of religious associations and surroundings, attended the Wesleyan Sunday school, at which he received a handsome bible as a reward for good conduct; and he enjoyed the high honour of not having caused his now bereaved father a moment's anxiety in his life as to his moral character.

During his mother's painful and protracted affliction, she evinced a strong preference for the affectionate and filial services in the sick room, of her only and much-loved son; and it is not unlikely that the experience of those years did much to make Richard the "handy" man he was in after days, and gave him singular aptness in ministering to the bodily as well as spiritual necessities of the afflicted and distressed.

If the child be the father of the man, Richard in early life was frank, cheerful, and exceptionally kind in disposition; earnest, plodding, and persistent in purpose; high and noble in aim; with a strong love for the beauties of nature, and an earnest desire to see and know what was going on in the world.

It was intended that he should follow a commercial life, and with this view he entered his father's place of business.

For the duties of this calling he had considerable aptitude; and had the original purpose of his friends been executed there was every prospect of a career of honourable and successful business enterprise before him, with a position of considerable social influence and usefulness in his native town. But, how often are human expectations cut off, and human arrangements frustrated!

> "There's a Divinity that shapes our ends
> Rough-hew them how we will."

And the Great Head of the Church had evidently reserved for our departed friend service in a higher and more arduous field, if for a briefer period.

The experience gained during his business life was of great service to him in his ministerial and missionary career; and fitted him to execute many matters requiring tact, foresight, and plodding energy, with credit to himself and advantage to the Church of God.

Section II.—Conversion.

Notwithstanding a boyhood marked, not only by the absence of vices so common in that period of life, but by the presence of numerous and conspicuous virtues, there was still the need of a personal religious life—a life springing from faith in Christ, controlled by love for Christ, and devoting, with unreserved consecration, all its powers to the service of Christ. This want was mercifully supplied in his sixteenth year. That most critical period of life, when habits are formed, companionships selected, and the course of life determined, was to him the time of religious decision. By an intelligent choice he elected to "put on the Lord Jesus Christ, and make no provision for the flesh, to fulfil the lusts thereof."

The circumstances of his conversion have been narrated by a companion—Mr. W. Cade; and from the account he has kindly furnished the following selections are made.

"I first became acquainted with the late Rev. R. S. Blackburn in the year 1863. In the August of that year I went to reside at Pontefract, and, being near neighbour to Mr. Blackburn, sen., I soon became acquainted with the whole of Mr. B.'s family, going in and out at any time almost as if it had been my home. At this time Richard was a pupil in Mr. R.'s school, and I remember attending some of the examinations, and finding he was not far from the head of the school, if not the top scholar. Some year or two after, he left school, and assisted his father in the business of ironmonger. I became more particularly acquainted with him at that critical time in the experience of every youth, when he begins to shape his course in reference to the future, with few or no fixed principles. I took him by the hand, and invited him to our class meeting, asking him to give his heart to God, and decide to live a Christian life. By the blessing of the Divine Spirit he hearkened to this advice, went with me to the class meeting, and the result was his speedy conversion to God.

"I do not know the exact date of his 'conversion,' or of his joining the church. I believe it was at home that he found peace with God, and I know it was not long after his first meeting in class. As near as I can remember it was in his sixteenth year. The class had a very good leader, and included many young people, especially young men, and we encouraged each other in good things. We had a list of prayer leaders connected with the society, and aimed at getting all the young men to join in the work of holding cottage prayer meetings in different parts of the town,— principally in the courts and alleys where sin abounded. To this list the name of R. S. Blackburn was soon added;

and thus was afforded to him an opportunity for the exercise of those gifts which shortly afterwards brought him into prominence as a preacher of the Gospel.

"I remember, also, soon after his conversion, he had a little room set apart for his own particular use; and we often used to meet there, for reading and prayer. Some of these were memorable seasons, and much spiritual power and joy were experienced by us."

Another correspondent, well acquainted with Mr. Blackburn as a youth, writes:—

"It is now about twelve years since I, as a child, first met Mr. B. According to my recollection of that time, he was naturally full of spirit, and warm-hearted where his sympathy was excited, and impetuous in manner. With a keen relish for the enjoyments of earth, and a strong desire to see all that he could of what was going on in the world, he might have been led astray, but for that power which drew his attention from worldly pleasures to the very highest blessings which a human being can enjoy. After he gave his heart to God, and received the witness of the Holy Spirit, he soon shewed signs of rapid growth in all that was good. He became almost rigid in habits of self-denial, and he was often thankful in after years for his early exercise of restriction."

Several interesting matters are indicated by the above communications.

Mr. Blackburn, as a youth, went to class on the kindly invitation of a friend and companion. Doubtless, many religious impressions had been made, and many religious desires awakened previously. The influence of the Sunday school, of the home, and of healthy social surroundings generally, were all favourable to a Christian choice; but the personal invitation of a friend brought these converging lines of influence to a focus, and led to prompt and decisive action. How largely we may and do influence each other for good or for evil! "No man liveth unto himself." What a mighty and beneficial power is friendship when sanctified to Christian purposes! How many young hearts have trusted in Christ, as the result of a friend's solicitude for their welfare! The invitations of the Gospel from the pulpit should be enforced and supplemented by personal, direct, affectionate appeal in private. How many might be won almost "by a word." Greater faithfulness by Christian people in this matter could hardly fail to yield most glorious results.

Our departed friend found Christ in seclusion and quietude. Variety marks equally the works of God in creation, and the operations of His grace in human enlightenment, and the culture of Christian character. Some hear the call of God in the hurricane and the tempest; others, in the gentle tones of the "still small voice." Some are aroused by the lightning and thunder of the law, in its menaces on the impenitent, of condemnation and ruin; others hear the "whispers of grace," and enter into life by processes gentle, persuasive, imperceptible:—the day dawns, the night of sin, indifference, and indecision terminates, as the "Sun of Righteousness" arises with healing in His wings; but the precise moment of spiritual illumination is difficult to determine. "The wind bloweth where it listeth, and thou hearest the sound thereof, but canst not tell whence it cometh, and whither it goeth: so is every one that is born of the Spirit." Some "press into the kingdom" in times of intense religious excitement, and are borne into the "haven of rest" on the crest of some tumultuous wave of "revival;" others glide into the harbour without noise, excitement, or observation. Some men's conversion is a moral rupture and convulsion: the debasing associations of years and decades are suddenly burst asunder; the chains forged by profligacy and vice are snapped; and the willing slave of appetite and passion leaps at once into "the liberty of the children of God." Other men's conversion produces no strongly marked change in their life and demeanour; the religious associations and training of home have prepared "the way of the Lord;" and they but reach the decision, and take the step to which all their previous life has been tending.

The conversion of any soul to Christ is an event of transcendent moment, and is fraught with issues the most blessed and far-reaching; but the conversion of some men is much more important than the conversion of others. Their powers are greater; their influence is mightier and more penetrating; and their service and success are more signal and complete. The conversion of a master-mind to Christ is often more momentous than the founding of a city, or the fate of a battle. What vast issues have arisen from the conversion of John Wickliffe, of Martin Luther, of John Wesley, of Charles H. Spurgeon! Such an event often creates eras, and produces revolutions in religious life and history. Mr. Blackburn's conversion was no isolated or trivial event in human life. It was the producing cause of a character of special excellence, and of a career of Christian service, brief indeed, but unusually devoted, energetic, and successful.

Mr. Blackburn promptly commenced the lifelong work of Christian culture. He had a room set apart for purposes of study and devotion; and deeply touching must have been those meetings of young men, of kindred spirit and aims, for fellowship and prayer. All the representations the Scriptures give us of the nature and obligations of Christian life, teach the necessity of growth in grace. It is not sufficient that a man be "born again." Birth anticipates progressive and unfolding life and powers. From infancy should be developed childhood, youth, and vigorous, mature manhood. He must walk before Christ "in newness of life." The few grains of corn in the husbandman's seed-basket have in them all the elements of a teeming harvest, but the beneficent forces of nature must bring them out; "first the blade, then the ear, then the full corn in the ear." The "leaven" placed in the measures of meal must "leaven the whole lump." The sin forgiven, the nature must be purified. The thoughts—the secret springs of action—must be "brought into captivity to the obedience of Christ;" the speech must be "that which is good to the use of edifying, that it may minister grace to the hearers;" and the whole conduct and life must be such as will "adorn the doctrine of God our Saviour in all things." It is not enough that we "put off the old man which is corrupt according to the deceitful lusts," we must "put on the new man which after God is created in righteousness and true holiness."

How necessary that new converts should realize vividly the necessity of Christian culture, and should use the Scriptural means of securing it! Prayer, private, regular, and earnest; Bible-reading, not only for purposes of instruction, but of devotion too; the "communion of saints," and the public worship of the sanctuary, are "means of grace," designed to form and foster spiritual life and character. How well Mr. Blackburn employed these "means," the entries in his diary conclusively prove.

"Every kind of life must be fed with the food which naturally agrees with it: animal, with material substances; intellectual, with intelligible propositions; and spiritual, with heavenly gifts. The first has sense for its instrument, the second reason, the third faith. Each rises above the other in importance and interest, though the whole are proper to the same being; and the perfection of all would be the perfection of the entire creature. Spiritual life is the noblest and best, and its instrument the most delicate and refined. Begotten by the Spirit, by Him it is fed; derived from Christ, through Christ it is preserved; and its food—the milk, and wine, and manna from above—is amply and richly supplied, through the means of grace."*

Mr. Blackburn began at once to work in the Lord's vineyard. He joined the band of Prayer-leaders. He saw that Christian life has its duties, as well as privileges, and must communicate, as well as receive, spiritual good. His was no selfish piety, always appropriating what will minister to its own interests, but seldom bestowing benedictions on others. He lived not to himself, but was solicitous to *do* the Master's will, and always ready "to spend and be spent" in the Master's service.

Work is a condition of all healthful life. Christ says to each one of us, "Son, go work to-day in My vineyard." And, probably, not a little of Mr. B.'s robust piety, and

---

* Dr. Stacey on "The Sacraments."

fruitful service, is traceable to the intensely practical character of his religious life.

In his twentieth year, he transferred his membership from Wesleyan Methodism to the Primitive Methodist Connexion. His reasons for this course seem to have been, appreciation of the zealous and aggressive spirit by which Primitive Methodism has ever been distinguished, coupled with the unconventional modes of operation by which its successes have sometimes been won; a preference for the emotional character, and spiritual fervour of its worship; and some difference of opinion with the leaders of the Wesleyan Church at Pontefract, on the Temperance question, and especially with reference to the use of fermented wine at the Sacrament of the Lord's Supper. These considerations he considered sufficient to determine his course; and there can be no doubt that he acted throughout the matter on Christian principle alone.

Rev. Hy. Crabtree, who was Superintendent of the Pontefract Circuit at the time Mr. Blackburn became a member of the Primitive Methodist Connexion, has contributed the following account of the event:—

"I became personally acquainted with our late brother, the Rev. R. S. Blackburn, in the early part of the year 1870. About that time he began to attend some of our public services at Pontefract, and occasionally visit the homes of some of our people. On one of these occasional visits, he gave me a private intimation that he would like to unite with us in Church-fellowship. From a sense of duty, I strongly urged him to remain among the people by whom he had been nursed and cradled from his childhood. He calmly replied, 'I cannot; my mind is made up. One of the leading officials has sharply snubbed me on account of my connection with the Temperance Society, and sympathy with the Temperance Reformation. I must have room for prudent action on that question, and cannot allow my personal liberty to be unduly restricted. Your people will aid, rather than hinder, me in all laudable endeavours to extend the cause of Temperance.'

"On April 8th, the leaders of the society at Pontefract adopted the following resolution :—'That a note be sent to the Rev. G. Rowe, Wesleyan minister, respectfully requesting him to favour us with Mr. R. S. Blackburn's credentials, as he is seeking admission into our Society, for reasons satisfactory to himself.' I saw Mr. Rowe personally, and handed to him a copy of the above resolution. He expressed his regret that Mr. Blackburn should think of leaving them, and spoke in commendatory terms of his sincerity and earnestness; and said, he hoped Mr. B. would be happy and useful among our people."

In matters of Christian doctrine, denominational character, spiritual aims, and, very largely, in methods of operation, Wesleyan and Primitive Methodism are identical. They differ in Church polity, though their differences are gradually being diminished by modifications which make each system approach the other. Historically, there are strong points of similarity, between these glorious and kindred religious revivals, though the one was seventy years anterior to the other. In both cases the "leaders" were men of unsullied lives, of burning zeal, and of tireless activity in the cause of Christ—men whose one mighty purpose was the glory of God in the salvation of their race. In both cases the religious movement, in its exuberance, burst open and overflowed the boundaries its promoters had fixed for it; and, like the fertilizing Nile on the soil of Egypt, brought life and beauty, fragrance and fruitfulness, wherever it came.

SECTION III.—CONSECRATION.

CHRISTIAN life may be considered in two aspects: in its inner principle of love, and faith, and zeal, and the right condition of heart and motive; and in its outer manifestation of excellence and service: the zeal finding its appropriate sphere; the faith evidencing itself in honest and hearty work; and the love budding forth into a bright and beautiful obedience.

Having chosen a religious life, and allied himself to the Church, Mr. Blackburn stedfastly aimed at growth in grace, and thus fitted himself for extensive usefulness in Christian service. His religion combined, in full proportions, the devotional and the practical. He regarded holiness of heart as the root from which spiritual fruitfulness must spring; and hence, his attention to the means of grace— private, social, and public—was regular, appreciative, and devout. He sat under the ministry of the Word with delight; and the 'fruit' of the sanctuary was sweet to his taste. He had deep practical sympathy with the Psalmist, when he exclaimed, "I was glad when they said unto me, let us go into the house of the Lord." And if prevented by indisposition or other causes from attending God's house, he was ready to say, "How amiable are Thy tabernacles, O

Lord of Hosts! My soul longeth, yea, even fainteth for the courts of the Lord: my heart and my flesh crieth out for the living God." He obeyed the Lord's injunction: "Take heed, therefore, how ye hear;" and was accustomed to note down in his diary the principal Scriptural truths that had been inculcated, and the aspects of Christian life discussed, in the discourses to which he had listened. Many such outlines of sermons, preached by the circuit ministers and others whom he occasionally heard, are before us as we write, and prove the attention he paid to the ordinances of the sanctuary, and the diligence with which he stored his mind with religious truth. Numerous extracts from his diary might be cited confirmatory of this aspect of his character.

There is one institution, peculiar to Methodism, which he prized most highly, and to which he gave devout and regular attention. This is the class meeting. Seldom was the week allowed to pass—and probably never without adequate reason—without his attendance at this eminently devotional and stimulating gathering of saints. The following selections from his diary illustrate this:—

July 29th, 1874.—"Attended class and had a blessed time."

Aug. 5th.—"At class we had a very powerful meeting. The Lord's presence was felt in large measure."

Aug. 12th.—"At class, our leader not being present, I had to officiate. The Lord was present, and blessed my soul with the refreshing influence of His Spirit. To me, indeed, it was good to be there."

Sept. 16th.—"Attended class—a blessed meeting; such a mellowing influence pervaded it. God is indeed blessing me this week. I will praise him. Christ is my refuge and strength, and present help."

Sept. 23rd.—"To-night at class was much blessed. My heavenly Father's love to me is indeed great. I cannot doubt His willingness to lead me through every difficulty, after He has so bountifully blessed me."

Oct. 21st.—"At night attended class—a blessed meeting; God was with us. In fact, I feel His presence hourly. My love for Him increases."

Nov. 11th.—"Our class to-night was well attended, and a gracious influence felt."

Dec. 23rd.—"At class enjoyed the Divine presence. No meeting gives me greater joy, or affords so much spiritual help."

The class meeting is an essential part of the institutions of Methodism; and one which we trust will never be allowed to fall into disuse. It has been a potent means of maintaining and developing spiritual life and power in the past; and, rightly used, will be so in the future. It is, in principle, if not in exact methods of procedure, old as Christianity itself. It has still power, under the Divine blessing, to sustain, comfort, and refresh. Often are these periodical gatherings of believers "times of refreshing" from the Lord's presence. They call forth gratitude, and recognise brotherhood; they elicit sympathy, and attest discipleship; and when the Father manifests his presence, Peter's exclamation on Mount Tabor is again heard: "Lord, it is good for us to be here." Much of the success of class meetings depends on the leader. He should be a man of unquestioned piety and prudence; his mind well stored with scriptural truth, and well acquainted with the workings of the human heart, and the various aspects of Christian experience : and thus be qualified to feed the flock committed to his care. Such a leader will

"Allure to brighter worlds and lead the way."

In the class meeting, Mr. Blackburn found the fellowship his social nature needed ; and, as we have seen, his religious life was thereby quickened and refreshed. He became a diligent student of the Divine Word ; and read also, with interest and profit, books on devotional, practical, and experimental religion—Wesley's Sermons, Cooke's Theology, Arthur's Tongue of Fire, Church History, and works of kindred character, being carefully perused. Some portion of each day was set apart for mental and moral culture. He was specially devotional in private; and received in consequence much of the Divine presence. He entered his "closet" and prayed to the "Father which is in secret ;" and the "Father, which seeth in secret," rewarded him openly.

The strength thus acquired in the means of grace, and by diligent personal culture, was devoted, without reserve, to purposes of practical beneficence. He was put on the preachers' plan ; and he strove most energetically to qualify himself for this important branch of Methodistic church work. Often was time redeemed from sleep during the week, in order to make suitable preparation for the pulpit on the Sabbath.

Probably no section of Christ's church surpasses Methodism in the manner in which it utilizes the "lay" agency within its fold. Methodism has been defined as

"Christianity in earnest;" and in the fulfilment of its high vocation, it must consecrate and employ every talent it possesses. In this hive there is no room for drones; but there is ample scope for the exercise of every faculty the church can command or acquire. Much of the success of Methodism must, undoubtedly, be attributed to the zealous and self-sacrificing labours of its " lay " or local preachers. This noble army has not only helped in the conquests gained, but has also largely defended the lines already won. It seems impossible that the work of Methodism could have been done without the devoted services of its lay ministry. It could not be done to-day; and the value and fitness of this agency have been long since demonstrated. Undoubtedly the quality of it might be, and ought to be, improved; and while strenuous efforts are being made to raise the standard of ministerial efficiency, it would be well to extend a helping hand to our useful and earnest band of local preachers.

Mr. Blackburn entered on this service with mind and heart; and such was his energy and faithfulness in it, that his " profiting " appeared "unto all." A few selections from his diary will show that he was by no means an unsuccessful toiler in this vineyard.

Feb. 8th, 1874.—" Walked to Normanton Common, and preached twice, with liberty and glorious results. Many professed to find peace."

Feb 22nd.—" Morning, attended service. Afternoon, visited sick and attended class. After tea went to the station with tracts, attended prayer meeting, and preached with liberty. Nine souls professed to find Christ."

March 29th.—"Afternoon walked to South Featherstone,

preached twice, and conducted an open-air mission ; spoke four times and laboured hard."

April 5th.—" Preached in the morning at Pontefract ; afternoon and night at Glass Houghton, with great liberty ; conducted open-air mission at five o'clock ; spoke twice. At prayer meeting, at night, there were six souls seeking Christ, and three professed to find Him."

May 3rd.—" Morning, at service ; afternoon, walked to Ackworth ; preached twice, and conducted out-door mission ; good services."

May 10th.—" Preached morning at Bentley ; and evening at Doncaster ; at five o'clock conducted out-door service, and spoke in the street ; six penitents at the prayer meeting."

May 17th.—" Morning and night attended service ; afternoon attended class, visited sick, and distributed tracts to the passengers at the station."

May 31st.—" Started, at 8 a.m., for camp meeting at Castleford ; preached in the morning ; processioned the streets afternoon and evening ; at night attended love-feast, and many professed to find the Lord."

June 14th.—" Morning walked to Knottingley camp meeting ; conducted the processions all day ; preached in the afternoon on the camp ground, and on the flat at five o'clock ; attended love-feast at night ; three converts."

Aug. 2nd.—" Attended and conducted camp meeting at Featherstone ; spoke several times in the processioning, and preached during the afternoon. Eight professed to find Christ."

Sept. 27th.—" Attended chapel in the morning ; afternoon walked to Ackworth ; preached twice, and conducted open-air service."

Oct. 4th.—"Preached at Brotherton, afternoon and evening, and conducted out-door mission; was much blessed in my work. Lord, save."

Oct. 18th.—"A blessed day to me; the missionary sermons were specially appropriate to my case, pointing me to foreign work."

Such are some of the entries in his diary for the year 1874; they are samples of many others that might be quoted, and they demonstrate the zeal, devotedness, and success by which his labours as a lay preacher were marked.

The closing page of his diary, each year, contains a summary of work and fruit in this service. The records for three consecutive years are as follows:—

1871.—"Preached forty-six times; walked 238 miles to my appointments; and have seen eleven conversions."

1872.—"Preached fifty-three sermons; walked 249 miles to my appointments; and have seen six conversions."

1873.—"Preached sixty-one times; walked 303 miles to my appointments; and have seen eighteen conversions."

These facts may be left to speak for themselves. So long as Primitive Methodism retains in the ranks of her lay ministry, men of such piety and zeal, her progress as a community is secured; and she has ample resources from which to fill her pulpits with "able ministers of the New Testament."

Many other departments of Christian and philanthropic work secured Mr. Blackburn's warmest sympathy and most cordial co-operation and support. To some of these incidental reference has been made. He had great delight in the distribution of religious tracts, and he ever kept himself well supplied with them; and he threw himself with great ardour into almost every form of Temperance work. He entered heartily into the Good Templar movement, and was raised to high office in that order in the locality in which he lived. An ardent abstainer himself, he assailed with characteristic energy the great vice of intemperance, and the liquor traffic generally, which he believed to be sapping the foundations of domestic happiness, national progress, and church prosperity. The maintenance of the institutions of the church, as the support of the ministry; the extension of Christ's kingdom by home and foreign mission work; and the erection, where needed, of suitable houses of prayer, received from him constant and generous support. Having first given himself to Christ, he gave time, toil, and treasure, without stint, to the demands of Christian service. "It is required in stewards that a man be found faithful;" and there seems little doubt that our revered friend exemplified, in an eminent degree, this cardinal virtue.

The following testimonies will confirm the foregoing statements, and illustrate Mr. Blackburn's singularly earnest piety, and devotion to every form of Christian work.

Rev. Hy. Crabtree writes:—"At the time he joined us we had a new chapel project in contemplation, and in the prosecution of the weighty undertaking we found him of very great service. When our people, to avoid expense, were spending their summer evenings—aided by many of their English and Irish neighbours—in removing the large house and other buildings, and the large and small fruit trees which occupied the site on which the present chapel and school are standing; and were preparing the old bricks and materials for the inner walls of the new buildings; and were digging out the foundations, to the depth of six or seven feet, by candle-light, till near the midnight hour; and were working till the dawn of day in the superintendent's house, preparing for a grand bazaar in aid of the building fund,—none, among the willing and praiseworthy toilers, worked more assiduously or cheerfully than our late dear brother. He thought it no self-degradation to throw off his coat and vest, and ply with vigour the pick, or spade, or hammer, or wheel a barrow, or do anything else which needed to be done. He also took a deep and active interest in the spiritual and numerical prosperity of the church, and often enquired if anything could be done to promote a revival of religion, and to ameliorate the moral condition of the degraded and drunken part of the population of the town. He kept himself well supplied with a good assortment of temperance and religious tracts and leaflets, and personally attended to their distribution among the people. He appeared to be never so happy as when in the act of doing good."

Another correspondent, who shared largely in the toil consequent on the erection of the chapel above referred to, writes thus:—

"When among the Wesleyans, he often visited our services, and impressed every one by his simple, fervent speech. The injunction, 'Whatsoever thy hand findeth to do, do it with thy might,' was literally fulfilled by him. Because purity, and truth, and justice were the laws of Christian life, he ever strove to inculcate a love of them in the hearts of those by whom he was surrounded in his business, and afterwards in the ministry; and, whenever he met with their opposites, under the garb of a Christian profession, he hurled against them, with all his might, the force of his disapprobation and aversion.

"When once decided as to the wrong or right of any principle or practice, he unflinchingly held to that which was right, whatever the opposition might be. He cultivated a strong sympathy with the interests of each life around him, and, wherever his help was needed, he was ready to give it cheerfully, willingly entering into the smallest joy or deepest grief of those who confided in him ; and it was at such times that he seized the opportunity for uttering a few words as to the blessedness of trust in God.

"After he had joined the Primitive Methodist Church, in Pontefract, and when the project for raising a new chapel was first begun, he entered into it at once, and was ready to do anything which would best serve its furtherance. He was appointed to several offices, all of which he attended to diligently. When he could not manage them without trespassing on business hours, he would cheerfully rise at four or five o'clock in the morning ; and he would often, in his thoughtfulness for others who were associated with him in the work, relieve them of little duties, where he saw too much was being attempted. Those days of hard work were very happy ones for the toilers ; for, though the effort was a great one, and the difficulties almost insurmountable, yet every one rejoiced in the union of spirit and oneness of aim which characterized the work of rearing their house of prayer ; and not soon will be forgotten the praises which went up from all the plodding ones, as they sung and prayed for the first time within its walls."

Mr. W. H. Hall, of Pontefract, who for many years was

acquainted with Mr. Blackburn, and a fellow-worker in the same circuit, writes thus:—

"The reminiscences of the years I have known Mr. Blackburn are of a very pleasant and encouraging character. I went to the same day school, the same Sunday school, and was connected with the same Band of Hope; so I had abundant opportunities of judging of his character and work. He was capable of very strong feeling, so that everything he undertook absorbed his whole soul; and to the furtherance of his purpose all must be subjected, no obstacle being too high to surmount, and no difficulty too great to be overcome. He joined the Band of Hope in 1863, in his thirteenth year; and from that time was a most energetic worker in the cause of temperance. He was a centre of interest and energy, and exercised a wide-spread influence, sparing no pains for the spread of the principles he prized so much.

"His work in the church was marked by great zeal and activity, by liberal contributions to all its institutions, and by regular attendance on the 'means of grace.' His religion was genuine—full of life, and power, and joy. He joined the Sunday school as a teacher; but his 'visiting' and pulpit labours demanded so much of his time, that he laid aside this work, though his interest and contributions still remained. He was a most excellent visitor; and by him many hungry ones have been relieved, and cheerless ones made glad. Many a time has he carried brightness into the almshouses and chambers of affliction. His reward is in heaven. I judge he was passionately fond of preaching, as it was to him a grand opportunity of publishing the tidings of salvation to lost man. His geniality of spirit—much developed by his religious life—made him acceptable wherever he went, and secured him many friends. As a young man, he filled a place and did a work which commanded the respect of all around him, reflected credit on himself, and which is rewarded by the permanence of the influence he exerts, and the glories of the world to come."

Rev. H. G. Hird, B.A., curate of Thornhill, contributes the following :—

" He was a young man of great earnestness, and took up work for God with much zeal and courage. Realizing the evils of desecrating the Sabbath, he did what he could to promote the better observance of that day ; and one means of his doing this was, to meet the trains at Pontefract station, and deliver tracts to the travellers.

" He strongly maintained his convictions of what he believed to be right. I have known him, at the sacrament of the Lord's Supper, refuse to receive the cup because the wine used was fermented. And he, as a total abstainer, thought that he ought not, even in that holy ordinance, to receive any wine except unfermented. In this I did not agree with him, but no persuasions could cause him to act otherwise.

" The Word of God was very much loved by him. His habit was, on retiring, to read a portion of Scripture as part of his devotions. By this means, he became deeply imbued with the true spirit of the Gospel. He realized deeply the presence of God, and cultivated the inner spiritual life. I have had several conversations with him on this part of the Christian's experience.

" The spirit of self-sacrifice was seen in him to a large extent; and thus it was that he was enabled to give up his business and a comfortable home, to preach the Gospel, not only among his own countrymen, but also to the Africans. I pray that others may be baptized with the same Spirit, and that they may earnestly carry on the work from which he was so soon taken away."

Rev. T. Baron, one of Mr. Blackburn's most intimate and esteemed friends, and who had special opportunities of studying his character and estimating his worth, furnishes the annexed appreciative remarks :—

"My acquaintance with Mr. Blackburn began in July, 1871, when I entered upon my work in the Pontefract circuit. During my stay in that circuit I enjoyed the hospitality of his father's house, and consequently was brought into close contact with our dear departed brother. From the first my attention was drawn to him, and I was instinctively led to admire and love him. At that time he was just beginning to preach, and manifested an earnest desire to become 'a workman that needeth not to be ashamed.' This desire did not evaporate in mere sentiment, but became a dominant practical force, and impelled him to conquer obstacles which would have been insuperable to many young men. His studies and preparations for the pulpit had to be attended to, in the brief intervals he could snatch from the rigorous requirements of the extensive and complicated business establishment with which he was connected. He spent very little time in sleep. Late to bed and early to rise was the rule with him.

"I saw that he was a young man certain to make his mark for good upon the town and neighbourhood in which he lived. He had been favoured with a respectable education; was endowed with good natural abilities; occupied an advantageous social position; determined to be of some use in the world; and yearned after complete dedication to God. He was always trying to do good. Work was a positive pleasure to him. Idleness would have been absolute misery. His temperament was ardent, even to the point of enthusiasm. His mental tendency was practical rather than speculative. While others would be sitting in their study, dreaming of the regeneration of society, and constructing fine but flimsy theories, our dear friend was out in the busy world, turning his hand to any and every form of practical philanthropy. It may surely be recorded of him, that what his hand found to do, he did it with his might. The amount of work he got through is simply amazing, and would have been impossible without very methodical habits, and constant self-sacrifice.

" His first efforts were, of course, directed to the interests of the church with which he had connected himself. He did no little towards raising Primitive Methodism, in Pontefract from the obscurity in which he found it, to its present position of respectability and influence. He threw himself heart and soul into the new chapel project. He did much evangelistic work, visiting the poor and the suffering, and acting as a true home missionary. Rain and storm never prevented him from keeping his appointments. He was no ecclesiastical dandy, flaunting himself in the sunshine. If there was any really hard and rough work to be done, Richard Stead Blackburn was ready to do it. Going to his appointments did not simply mean preaching in the place provided to whomsoever would come and hear him; it meant going out into the highways and hedges, and compelling people to come in. During the intervals of service he was accustomed to visit from house to house, speak a cheery word of invitation, and leave a silent messenger of mercy. He would often take his stand on some village green, or door-step, and cast the seed of life upon the waters. He was specially at home in these effective methods of reaching the masses.

"In addition to his evangelistic work, he was much engaged in earnest temperance toil. He saw intemperance blighting the manhood of the people, undermining social stability, and impeding the progress of Christianity, and at once set himself to do what he could to destroy the evil. He was one of the most enthusiastic and prominent temperance reformers in Pontefract, and did much towards creating some temperance societies and consolidating others. He was also active in political affairs, and laboured hard to promote the cause of Liberalism. He was an enlightened and active citizen of earth, as well as a devout and zealous citizen of heaven. In fact, there was every probability of his becoming one of the leading laymen of the Pontefract circuit; but the Great Head of the Church destined him to other work in wider spheres."

CHAPTER II.

Chosen Sphere.

"Son, go work to-day in My vineyard."—*Jesus.*
"The love of Christ constraineth me."—*Paul.*
"The essence of true nobility is neglect of self. Let the thought of self pass in, and the beauty of a great action is gone, like the bloom from a soiled flower."

THE office of the Christian preacher is of Divine appointment, and, when worthily sustained, is one of peerless dignity and commanding influence. There is no other office among men calculated to produce results so important and far-reaching. The practice of the law, contributing to the maintenance of justice, the conviction of crime, and the vindication of innocence, is important and beneficial; so is, also, the practice of medicine, alleviating human suffering, promoting health, and extending life; so is, also, the labour of the legislator, creating, arranging, and enforcing wise, just, and beneficent laws. The pursuit of commerce is honourable in itself, and immensely promotive of human welfare, in the capital it creates, and in the employment it affords to millions of the human race; suggesting the time when "there shall be no complaining in our streets," and "when our garners shall be full, affording all manner of store." The pursuit of literature, when properly directed, is an incalculable boon, as it stimulates thought, enlarges the range of intellectual vision, and contributes to the formation and elevation of character. But all these are secondary to the "ministry of the Word," and cannot compare with the work of preaching the "everlasting Gospel." The divinely appointed preacher dwells on loftier themes, aims at nobler objects, and produces results more momentous and enduring than any of these, or all combined. He has to do not only with the physical, mental, and social surroundings of man, but with his inner, spiritual, eternal nature. He has to announce to man truths, and to bring to bear upon him influences, spiritual and divine; which not only bless him in time, but prepare him for eternity. He is an "ambassador for Christ," with terms of mercy from the court of heaven to the rebels of earth; and, at his Master's command, and in his Master's "stead," beseeches men to be "reconciled to God." He has to take the "unsullied and eternal truths of God," and, in the language of living men, speaking them to his fellows, "turn men from darkness unto light, and from the power of Satan unto God." He has to lead men from the false to the true, from the wrong to the right, from the sinful to the pure, from all that is worldly, carnal, and selfish, to all that is noble, spiritual, and divine. His one grand business is, to make men better; through the individual, to promote the moral and spiritual refinement and elevation of the human race; and, in all the relations of life, to sanctify and ennoble man's whole nature. Such is the magnificent calling of the Christian preacher! And, in the accomplishment of his work, he has the truth of God for his instrument, man for his audience, and the power of the Holy Spirit to guarantee success.

The qualifications for a work so responsible and glorious

are of such a character as only the "Great Head of the Church" can bestow. Every true minister is himself the subject of renewing grace, and has his own heart deeply affected by the power of Christ. Nothing can compensate for the lack of this. He may have learning and eloquence, he may have zeal and fervour; but if a preacher be not personally and eminently holy, he will seldom be " mighty to the pulling down of strongholds." It is necessary to lay hold of every appliance within our reach. A thorough and extensive knowledge of the truths of theology is requisite. A keen insight into, and a comprehensive acquaintance with the human heart is immensely valuable; but high above these, is the prime requisite of personal consecration :—of personal contact with Christ, of personal conversion to God, and santification through the Spirit. Who can set forth the soul's deep need of Christ, but the man who has felt it? Who can sing of mercy like him who has obtained mercy? Who can teach the way to the cross, but he who has travelled it? Who can gratefully and urgently proclaim the joy of pardon, but the man who has experienced that joy in his own heart? This fact explains why the ministry of some men, of very ordinary powers and endowment, is so mighty in the influence it exerts, and the results it secures. The presence of Christ in them is the source of their power. A vivid realization of the blessings of the Gospel in their own hearts is the secret of their success in preaching the Gospel to others. And thus, fired by an intense love to Christ, having an unflinching faith in His Gospel, and an ardent desire for His glory, in "words that burn" they "tell the story of the Cross," till the glow of their own religious fervour communicates itself to other hearts, and awakens a response there, and they become efficacious witnesses and preachers of the Lord Jesus Christ. The seraphic piety of Fletcher of Madeley, the flaming zeal of Whitfield, the quenchless love of Brainerd, and the intense devotedness of Payson, were preludes to their vast and pre-eminent usefulness.*

Methodism obtains her ministers from the ranks of her *local* preachers—those who have proved their piety and faithfulness, by years of previous and arduous service, and have demonstrated their ability to preach with efficiency, by the results that have crowned their efforts. We have seen how Mr. Blackburn passed through this preliminary stage in the life of a Methodist preacher; with what exemplary diligence he prepared for his pulpit efforts; with what intense missionary zeal his preaching excursions in the villages around his native town were marked; and with what "signs" of divine sanction in the conversion of sinners, his services were accompanied. We must now consider him in that critical juncture of his life when he heard, in the call of the church, the call of God, to take upon himself " the ministry of the Lord Jesus," and consecrate time, talent, and strength wholly to that sublime service.

In the appointment of a Methodist minister the candidate must have approved himself to the congregations to which he has already ministered, "a workman that needeth not to be ashamed, rightly dividing the word of truth;" he must be recommended to this office by the suffrages of his brethren in Quarterly Meeting assembled; he must be examined on matters of personal religion, on his knowledge of Scriptural truths, and as to his general intelligence, by a board of senior

---

*H. W. Beecher.

ministers, whose acknowledged abilities and experience have given them the confidence of the church; and having passed these tests, he is "recommended" either for immediate "active work" in the ministry, or for a term of theological and literary training in the Colleges.

The subjoined quotations from Mr. B.'s diary, indicate his strong desire for divine guidance in this matter of supreme moment :—

Sept. 7th, 1874.—"Have been the subject of very much conflict, mentally, but am trying to be passive in God's hands, knowing He will lead me aright."

Sept. 14th.—"Our Quarterly Meeting at Castleford. I was unanimously recommended for the ministry, but not having light clear enough, I could not consent. 'Oh, my Father! teach me Thy will, and help me to do it.'"

Sept. 15th.—"I have this day had a blessed experience; such a giving up of self, and a baptism of God's love as I never felt before. The Lord will lead me."

Sept. 16th.—"Attended class; a blessed meeting; such a hallowing influence pervaded it. God is indeed blessing me this week. I will praise Him. Christ is my refuge and strength, and present help."

Sept. 23rd.—"To-night at class was much blessed; my heavenly Father's love to me is indeed great, during my trial. I cannot doubt His willingness to lead me through every difficulty, after He has so bountifully blessed me."

A few months later he writes—

Feb. 1st, 1875.—"We had a splendid sermon from the President to-night, to whom I was introduced. He gave me much help by saying, 'Hold to it; be faithful and you will win!' referring to my call to the ministry. Lord help me!

Thou art my strength, and 'my exceeding great reward.' 'Bless the Lord, O my soul, and forget not all His benefits.' 'The Lord of Hosts is with me; the God of Jacob is my refuge.' 'I will sing unto the Lord; I will praise Him for ever.'"

Feb. 11th.—"Attended the prayer meeting, but lacked faith; therefore was not so much blessed as I might have been. The conflict still rages. The body takes much bringing into a state of subjection."

Feb. 13th.—"Have been brought much nearer to God; I feel His power resting upon me, but still I want more fixedness of purpose."

Feb. 14th.—"The Lord blessed me much whilst delivering His Word at Brotherton to-day, and especially while visiting the sick. I delight in His work."

Feb. 21st.—"To-day I preached to the noisest and most enthusiastic congregation I ever addressed; and was much blessed; and yet I do not realize the 'fulness' of blessing for which I long. Lord, save me fully!"

In addition to earnestly seeking Divine guidance, at this important period of his life, Mr. Blackburn sought the advice of his friends. Some of his letters, at this time, are now before us, and they confirm the statements of his diary, that he was solely anxious to know God's will in the matter. The following letter to the Rev. W. B. Luddington, then rendering his first term of service as a Missionary in Fernando Po, is an interesting reminiscence of this period; and is, moreover, suggestive, as indicating the bent of the writer's mind even then, in regard to Foreign Missionary work.

"*Pontefract, Sept.* 29*th*, 1874.

"MY DEAR FRIEND,

"You will be rather surprised to hear from me on the question on which I now write. I have been passing through a very severe conflict during the last month; and the importance of the subject must be my excuse for troubling you, as, doubtless, your time will be very fully occupied.

"For a long time I have been impressed with the idea that I ought to be in the ministry, but have kept these thoughts to myself. About six months ago, the Rev. J. G. L—— asked me to allow him to mention me as a suitable person for the ministry. I then refused, on the ground of my usefulness as a layman. Three months later he renewed his request. I again refused; feeling, however, somewhat condemned. A week before last quarterly meeting, he urged the matter upon me again. I felt I dared not say, 'don't mention it;' but, at the same time, I could not say the call was Divine, until I had more satisfactory evidence. At the quarterly meeting, the subject was brought up and discussed, and I was unanimously recommended. I, however, declined to allow the recommendation to be forwarded to the Connexional authorities, as the light I then had was not clear enough. Feeling the importance of the crisis, I determined not to move until the Spirit took hold of me more powerfully, and revealed His will, so that I could not make a mistake.

"When I reached home, I told father all about it, and asked him to look at the matter calmly and prayerfully. I then retired to my room, and earnestly sought to know the Lord's will. I laid my all—wealth, body, and soul—before Him; and, while offering the sacrifice, God revealed Himself to me, and I felt immediately that it was His will that I should go. In addition to this direct working of the Spirit in favour of my going, He has worked indirectly. The sermons I have since heard, the hymns that have been sung, the advice of my dearest Christian friends—all have pointed in the same direction.

"Temporally considered, the work is not to be desired; my present position is, as I have every comfort; but the Lord's will is more to me than all these things. You will forgive me troubling you with so many of the details of my call; I wish you to know, as one having passed through it, that you may be better able to advise.

"It is possible, at some future day, the Lord might want me for foreign work. If He should, how am I to decide? Will you kindly tell me a few of the details of your call to Africa? I should not like to go to any field of labour unsent; nor should I like to grieve the Spirit by refusing to go.

"You will doubtless be writing to some of your friends by next mail; and I should be very grateful for a line enclosed.

"Hoping you may be blessed with increasing success in your labours,

"Your sincere friend,

"R. S. BLACKBURN."

The next letter was written to a young friend, a few months prior to his entrance upon the work of the ministry; and evinces an intense desire to know something of the "higher life," in order that he might have the investiture "of power," as a preparation for his glorious calling.

"*Pontefract, Jan.* 27th, 1875.

"DEAR BROTHER HEWITT,

"I feel the weight of my future work upon me. My inefficency as a preacher troubles me considerably. I seem to lack the necessary qualifications; and yet, such is the clearness of my call, that I dare not refuse to go.

"What are your views on *entire* sanctification? I desire to know what it is, and to experience it. Is it a gradual or an instantaneous work? How can it be obtained? Do you possess it? If so, how did you get it? I am convinced it will bring the power we need, in order to be successful in the glorious work we have undertaken. Oh! for the baptism of *fire!* Oh! for the power of the Holy Ghost! Let us pray, my brother, that it may descend on the hearts of our young ministers, that we may be burning and shining lights in this dark world.

"Yours very fraternally,

"R. S. BLACKBURN."

There is another event which is so *closely* associated with Mr. Blackburn's call to the ministry, and which, probably more than any other event, influenced for good his character and labours, that reference must be made to it. For some time previous he had entertained a strong and pure affection for a devoted and gifted young lady, in every way worthy of the deep regard he had for her. Their intercourse did not ripen into a formal engagement till the momentous decision to resign commercial pursuits and enter the ministry was reached; and the correspondence of this period reveals more clearly than anything else, the noble and disinterested motives which prompted his choice and course. In his perplexity he naturally turned for counsel to the friend esteemed above all others, and on whose goodness and judgment he placed implicit reliance.

We select the following letters for insertion here:—

"*Pontefract, Sept. 7th,* 1874.

"MY DEAR ——

"I have been asked by Mr. L—— to offer myself for the ministry, and expect the Quarterly Meeting next Monday will also call. I should very much like your opinion and advice before giving a final answer. . . I am in darkness, not knowing which way to move. If you can shed any light upon my path, I shall be very grateful. I desire to do right; wealth and other worldly considerations do not weigh with me at all; but I tremble lest I should do wrong. A false step now, who can tell the consequences?

"I feel quite alone in the world, no one to whom I can go for advice. If I ask . he will advise interestedly; and the majority of people look at things from a monetary point of view; so I think you will forgive me for laying this matter before you, and also favour me with a reply."

To the above letter he received the following answer:—

"*Sept.* 11*th*, 1874.

"MY DEAR FRIEND,

"My hope is, that in answer to our prayers, your mind is somewhat at rest by this, or will be by the time when this shall reach you. Shall I tell you, first of all, that up to now I have dreaded any one of my friends being called to the ministry? I am ashamed to acknowledge it, yet it has been so. I have always counted it a great honour to be engaged in a work so glorious; but it has been associated with so much self-denial and suffering that I have entertained a fear of it, and cherished a hope that   might be the only one among my circle of friends whose life should be given up to the work, and his only, because he was already in it. It is, perhaps, that I have felt so deeply the sacrifices and heavy trials which   had to bear, all of which have seemed to be connected with the lot they had chosen. The remembrance of them has always been painful, except when I have thought of the way in which God has brought them through, and that last ought never to have been forgotten. Strange to say, it has had a powerful effect in strengthening my trust in God,—the knowledge of what He has done for them—but I have not thought of the two things together, as I should have done. Since being very young I have known most of the early life of   more than any other besides themselves have known—and as I have pondered it over, I have grown to regard it as being very different from what might have been, had they chosen a different lot, again forgetting God's being over all. Looking at it now, it seems strange to me that I should have been so blind. I firmly believe that God has a certain work for each, and it does not matter what there may be attendant on *that work*, of joy or sorrow, of ease or pain, wealth or poverty, God has appointed it, and it is *infinitely best* for us. It seems to me very wrong to weigh over the advantages or disadvantages of a certain thing, and having decided which is best, in a worldly point of view, to act accordingly. Rather leave ourselves in God's hands, and He will make it plain. I believe one may, in part, judge from surrounding circumstances what His will is. In your case it seems hard to tell. It seems as though you were, in your present work, likely to do great good. With the disposition to give and work, and doing it as for God, you might be a great power in His hands. But then, in your direct work for Him, you have, I suppose, met with marked success. Of course this will weigh with you most. You are, no doubt, thinking that you might and would be able to do far more good if you gave up your whole time and strength to it. It might be so, and it might not. The Church is not infallible, and I believe often errs in her calls to the work. I should say that, unless your own heart is leaning very much to the work, that it were better to remain as you are. In saying this, I do not wish you, if you think differently, to be influenced in the least by it.

"*I have prayed earnestly* for you, but principally that you might *yourself* see what you ought to do. I have prayed that I might say nothing which should guide you in the wrong direction, but I believe that direct light will be given you, and so I pray. I say wait, until you see clearly, and do not respond to the call if you do not feel perfect confidence. God has put you in your present work, and do not for a world of impulses stir out of it, unless in calm dependence on Him you feel that He calls you elsewhere. If this is the case, and you do feel assured that it is God himself who calls, then, I say, go forth to the work, and the Lord be with you. Heed not what family or friends may say, God is over all, and will supply all your need; and if there should be in your path many thorns, or much trial, never forget what I have sinfully forgotten, *God has ordained it so*, and He will watch over you; you will never have more than you can bear.

"I would, though, determine at once, that it should be all work or none. There are so many half-hearted workers, men who start out with plenty of zeal, but who gradually lose it, and become intent only on being popular, or in getting through nicely, doing work that comes to their hands, but never seeking it.

"If, as it may be, you are still in darkness, or feel persuaded that your work is to be in your present sphere, I would say, do not trouble, and think that you are in the wrong. It would be well, I think, to determine afresh that all you have and are shall be given up to His service, and the Lord be with you in it.

"Oh, I think there are none on all the earth so rich and blessed as those who have God's love in their hearts, and the wonder to me is that we should rest content with so little. So *much* within reach, and yet so *little* in our possession."

In a second letter on Sept. 14th, 1874, he wrote—

"You have faithfully laid before me some of the disadvantages attending the work of the ministry, and now that the crisis has come, I am obliged to look these things fairly in the face. But as I do so I am reminded they must not influence me in my decision. I do thank you from my heart for the prayers you have offered on my behalf; and whichever way I may decide, I shall remember these prayers; they will strengthen me in the future.

"Now as to my own views on the subject when I first wrote you. I thought how useful I might be at home. There is a great call for intelligent laymen. I have been moderately useful in the Church, and in the Temperance movement. My social position gave weight to my influence, and my business abilities are such that I probably should have improved that position. These things were weighing with me considerably. But there is another side to the question. The ministry offers scope for usefulness, such as could not be found elsewhere. A true minister of the gospel wields an influence such as no other person can; and if I could import my zeal and energy, together with piety into it, and be baptized by the Holy Ghost, no one can tell the amount of good I should accomplish. My circumstances too seem to be thrusting me out, and many things combine to indicate that God is requiring me for this work. Many friends have the impression that I ought to go. The Quarterly Meeting *unanimously* recommends me. Yesterday morning's sermon (by an entire stranger) was on Jonah's refusal to go to Nineveh. I have named the matter to my father tonight, and the only objection he raises is one of business. The happiest moments of my life have been spent in the pulpit, and my love for God's cause is intense.

"I am looking at these two phases of the matter, and as I gaze I await divine guidance, which I am persuaded will be granted. Nor do I lose sight of the sacrifices which have to be made if I go. There are hundreds of comforts which I now have which cannot be purchased by a Primitive Methodist Minister's salary; there is the prospect of comparative poverty for life; there is the snapping of many social ties; there is incessant physical and mental exertion; and worse than all, I fear, from the tone of your letter, I should have to relinquish your heart and hand. But, notwithstanding all this, if the Lord clearly and distinctly says go, I cannot refuse, I must not stay. My chief fear is lest I be led by some wrong motive; but I feel as though many prayers had been offered on my behalf, and my own intercourse with the Father is sweet."

Other communications followed, and ceaseless prayer for divine guidance was offered, till at last the finger of God was seen to clearly indicate the ministry as the providential path. The dark night of uncertainty and perplexity, of anxious thought and conflicting influences, was followed by the welcome day of assured peace and guidance for the present, and calm and courageous trust in God for the future. Two hearts—each "willing to do the will of God"—were singularly united in the one sublime act of self-surrender to God and His work. Seldom has the devotion of two souls to each other been made to hinge so completely on the supreme devotion of each to Christ. The sacrifice asked was the unreserved surrender of all prospects of earthly gain, position, and influence to the great cause of God and the interests of mankind; the blessing given was "peace that passeth understanding," a "joy unspeakable and full of glory," a realization of divine love richer than ever before known, and a confidence in God that set at rest the perturbations of anxious hearts, and that filled the future with brightness and promise. Mr. B. writes: "I cannot tell you the holy joy and peace of the last few days.

I have indeed experienced what I have long sought in the religious life; and, oh, how sweet it is! No will of my own, for it is lost in God's." And he is answered: "I feel the quiet one knows after a storm, and my trust in God is strong. This trial has been to me harder than any I have had before, but I think the result is that God and His work are dearer to me now than they have ever been. I am quite humbled with the humility which comes from God. I do not fear what there is in the future for me. *God is my friend*, and I am praying every day for *perfect peace*."

Reference is made in one of Mr. Blackburn's letters to a sermon preached by one who was a stranger to his circumstances, and while he was in uncertainty as to his course in life, on "Jonah's refusal to go to Nineveh;" and so remarkably was the sermon applicable to his own case that he was much moved. The preacher on that occasion—the Rev. George Warren—has kindly furnished me with the following account of the service:—"I remember the service at Pontefract very well. I was going to preach anniversary sermons at another place in the circuit, but was making my home in the town, at Mr. Blackburn's. I was requested to preach in the Pontefract Chapel on the Sunday morning before going out to my afternoon and evening's work in the country. The service was very enjoyable, and I have seldom felt more solemnity and hope than at that time. I cannot give you an outline of my sermon, as it was only an extemporaneous comment on the early part of Jonah's history, and was not divided in any orderly fashion. I remember that the portion of the discourse which seemed to be accompanied with the greatest influence was that in which I was trying to show that our conduct in relation to the important calls of the

Lord, very often decides the character of our whole after life. After the service an experienced female met Mr. Blackburn in the porch, and told him that the sermon was for him, and he said in reply that he knew it was. He spoke to me in similar terms on the subject, and said he thought he would have to give himself up to the work. What I said in the sermon was only in the style of simple conversation, and the effect was due entirely to the gracious influence which was so richly felt during the service, and not by any means to my commonplace words."

During Mr. Blackburn's perplexity as to his work in life, he asked God to give him special directions one night on his knees, and with his bible before him, by impressing on his mind suitable and suggestive portions of Holy Scripture ; and the following, among others, speedily came under his notice :—

"The harvest truly is plenteous, but the labourers are few. Pray ye therefore the Lord of the harvest, that he will send forth labourers into His harvest."—Matt. ix. 37, 38.

"He that loveth father or mother more than Me is not worthy of Me ; and he that loveth son or daughter more than Me is not worthy of Me. And he that taketh not his cross, and followeth after Me, is not worthy of Me. He that findeth his life shall lose it : and he that loseth his life for My sake shall find it."—Matt. x. 37-39.

"For what is a man profited if he shall gain the whole world and lose his own soul ? or what shall a man give in exchange for his soul ?"—Matt. xvi. 26.

"And every one that hath forsaken houses, or brethren, or sisters, or father, or mother, or wife, or children, or lands, for My name's sake, shall receive an hundredfold, and shall inherit everlasting life."—Matt. xix. 29.

"Go ye, therefore, and teach all nations, baptizing them in the name of the Father, and of the Son, and of the Holy Ghost."—Matt. xxviii. 19.

This was sufficient; and fully convinced, he decided to give up all and follow his Master. After that, nothing could move him from his purpose. He often trembled at the thought of his own insufficiency and lack of knowledge, and felt afraid of the greatness of the work to which he was called, but he steadily sought for faith in the one whose strength was promised for all his need.

There can be no doubt that in entering the ministry, Mr. Blackburn acted from the highest and purest motives. Influences of no ordinary character urged him to decline the call, to pursue a career of energetic and successful business enterprise, and to fill a position of usefulness, respectability, and honour, as a lay worker in the church; but when once God's voice was heard calling him to His service, he "conferred not with flesh and blood," but joyfully entered on the momentous work. He felt that to do God's will was his chief desire, and that to spend the whole of his time and strength in His service would give him greater joy than the accumulation of worldly store.

Rev. T. Baron writes, "He was called to the regular ministry in 1875. His correspondence with me at that time indicated the clearness and emphasis with which that 'call' came to his soul, and his readiness to respond to it, whatever sacrifice it might involve. He was concerned only for the glory of God. 'Lord! what wilt Thou have me to do;' 'Here am I, send me;' are the mottoes which most appropriately express the attitude of his spirit at this critical juncture of his life. After severe heart-searching, fervent prayer, and correspondence with his friends, he decided to give himself fully to the Christian ministry. He did not ask to be put into the Priests' office for a piece of bread. He did not enter the ministry because he could not succeed in business. He was on the highway to wealth when the call came, and freely gave up all chance of making a fortune to become a Methodist preacher."

Ordinarily, a course of preparatory training is given to candidates for the ministry, the term being longer or shorter as circumstances dictate; but sometimes a man is taken direct from manual or mercantile pursuits and appointed to the ministerial office. The latter course was a necessity in the early days, and for a long period in the history of the Primitive Methodist Connexion. The character of the work, the paucity of means, the needs of the times, with other causes, prevented anything like a systematic mental and theological training being given to Primitive Methodist ministers for many years. Nor did the peculiar character of the work they had to do require so urgently as might be supposed the training of the "Schools." Large intellectual attainments in the ministry are certainly very desirable acquisitions. This is especially so as congregations advance in social position and mental culture. It has been said, that if God has no need of men's knowledge, he has no need of men's ignorance; and the minister, in mental culture and resources, should be somewhat in advance of the generality of his congregation. The work of the ministry admits of the most splendid talents, and the ripest culture, being employed in its service, and consecrated on its altar. It will welcome and utilize the richest gifts, whether of mind or of speech; it will accept and ennoble the deepest and most extensive knowledge; and it will find ample scope for the largest and most varied stores of intellectual and spiritual wealth and attainment, if consecrated by the Spirit of God and prayer. But while this is admitted and defended, it must also be granted, that there are some departments of this work where such qualifications are not absolutely necessary to efficiency or success.

Such was the work done by the preachers in the earlier years of the history of Primitive Methodism. They laboured for the most part among the masses of our working population, who were generally illiterate, and often degraded people. Fine intellectual sermons would have been of little service among the audiences they addressed. Learned disquisitions on controverted points of doctrine would have been useless, or worse. Nicely rounded periods of eloquence cast in classic mould, and spiced with classic lore, would have found no abiding place in the memories, and made no impression on the hearts of the depraved masses who listened to their words. Successful toilers in such a field must be men of deep and vivid religious experience, with lively and stirring religious exercises; men with a good general knowledge of the truths of the gospel, and with tongues fluent in uttering and enforcing them; men with hearts all aglow with love to God and man, burning with zeal for the divine glory in the conversion of souls, and ready to do, and dare, and die in the Master's service; such men were likely to reach, impress, and save the masses of our population, and such men were the pioneers of the Primitive Methodist Connexion. They were men mighty in prayer and faith, dauntless in courage, and tireless in toil; and were much more anxious about breaking sinners' hearts than they were afraid of breaking the rules of logic or grammar. It should be remembered, however, to their honour, that not a few, in spite of almost incessant ministerial labours, have, by their industry in mental culture and toil, taken respectable rank among the educated and literary men of their day.

It is a law of Christian life that it shall produce not only spiritual, but mental, social, and material results of marked character. Christian truth enjoins diligence, integrity, prudence, sincerity, transparency of character, speech, and aim; all of which tend to promote temporal prosperity. They form a character to be trusted; they invite confidence; and they often lead to signal commercial success, and to elevated social position. "Seest thou a man diligent in business, he shall stand before kings, he shall not stand before mean men." "Not slothful in business, but fervent in spirit, serving the Lord."

And the principle so palpably operative in individual life, manifests itself in the collective life of a Christian community. In the nature of the case there must be advancement in intelligence, in social influence, and in material prosperity. Doubtless, piety and poverty are often found inhabiting the same abode; but ordinarily the intimacy will not be of very long duration, and ultimately the piety will expel the poverty, and introduce social comfort in its place. And so it comes to pass that communities reputed to be "poor" and "illiterate" grow "intelligent," and, as the phrase goes, "respectable." The fact is, the change is natural and inevitable. Given, fidelity to privilege and duty, and nothing can check the upward and onward movement to intelligence, influence, and position. Primitive Methodism is no exception to this general law; and the spacious sanctuaries it is rearing, the Colleges and other educational institutions it is founding, and the growing intelligence of its congregations, demand, and are fed by, the advancing culture of its ministry.

It is devoutly to be wished, that this educational movement should be accompanied by no decay in the fervour of piety and service which has marked the life of the community in former days. In the introductory Lecture to "Systematic Theology," by the late and revered Rev. John Petty—the first conferentially appointed Theological Tutor of Candidates for the Primitive Methodist Ministry—this danger is noticed, and suitable counsel given respecting it. He furnished, in his own ministry, one of the finest examples of supreme devotedness to God that Methodism has produced; and he did much by the intensity of his piety, as well as by the wisdom of his teachings, to foster an intense thirst for the enduement of power the baptism of the Holy Ghost gives. "Think," said the now sainted minister, to the young men entrusted to his care, "of the noble examples which are left on record on the page of history. Consider the faith and courage of Peter on and after the day of Pentecost, the quenchless zeal of Paul, and the perfect, overflowing love of John. And, to come to modern times, contemplate the ardour of Baxter; the melting compassion of Brainerd; the apostolic zeal and labours of Wesley; the tenderness and power of Whitfield; the seraphic piety of Fletcher; and the eminent holiness of numerous others, both in the early and later days of Methodism. Forget not the noble example of the fathers and founders of our own Connexion; the self-denying and laborious course of Bourne; the lofty piety and extraordinary success of Clowes; the wondrous faith and usefulness of Oxtoby; the devoted labours of Batty, Belham, and others: some gone to their reward, and some still left to bless a little while longer the militant church below, but almost daily expecting the summons to join the church triumphant above. O that the mantles of our ascending Elijahs may fall upon our young Elishas! And *why* may not *you*, my brethren, catch the falling mantles of our ascending fathers? You may not *all* indeed expect to equal *some* of them in preaching talents, and other useful gifts; but if you improve your religious privileges aright, you may all equal, if not surpass, the most distinguished of our fathers in religious attainments. Remember that you have an interest in the same Saviour as they had, the same means of access to God, the same promises of grace to encourage you, and the same blessed Spirit to help you. Pray, then, for great things through the mediation of your all-sufficient Redeemer; expect large things through His infinite merits; and according to your faith it shall be done unto you."

Mr. Blackburn was sent *direct* to the work of the ministry. That a course of preparatory training would have been a great boon to him, none would have been more ready to admit than himself; but his previous education, general intelligence, observant mind, business experience, and regular habits of study, made the lack of it less felt than it otherwise might have been. He left his native town to commence his great life-work, full of high hopes of earnest and faithful service in the Master's vineyard, and cheered by the warm sympathy and prayers of his friends. The following testimony is borne by her who had consented to be his help-meet in the great service, to the singularly

Christian tone of his spirit at this time. "The beginning of our more intimate friendship was marked by important changes in our lives and prospects, and I can never forget the earnest prayer that was offered to God, as we knelt together at that time imploring His blessing on our intercourse with each other; that we might never seek our own happiness alone, but that we might do the perfect will of God. As the prayer went up a sweet assurance came to us that we should be led safely by our Father, and we never lost it afterwards."

CHAPTER III.

Faithful Toil.

"I must work the works of Him that sent Me while it is day: the night cometh, when no man can work."—*Jesus.*

"This one thing I do."—*Paul.*

"The true ambition there alone resides
Where justice vindicates and wisdom guides,
Where inward dignity joins outward state,
Our purpose good, and our achievements great."—*Dr. Young.*

Section I.—Bingley.

BINGLEY is a busy and thriving manufacturing town in Yorkshire, of about twelve thousand inhabitants. It is situated on the banks of the Aire, and is surrounded by landscape scenery of great beauty. Nicholson, the Airedale poet, thus speaks of some of the natural features of the locality:—

"When on thy lovely vale I stand to gaze,
I feel thou need'st from me no meed of praise;
Thy hanging woods, thy fountains and thy bowers,
Thy dashing floods, thy landscapes and thy flowers,
Thy bold grey rocks, thy heathy purple fells,
Where silent solitude with beauty dwells;
Thy homes where honest worth still finds a seat,
And love and virtue a serene retreat—
Such scenes as these shall plume the poet's wing,
And swell his heart while he attempts to sing.

Faithful Toil.

> We have the mountain breeze, the cold pure spring;
> The woods where every British bird doth sing;
> Wild plants and flowers, wild birds, and scenes as wild,
> Or soft, as any on which nature smiled;
> Blooming and lovely, as the moon is fair,
> And pure as ether, are the nymphs of Aire.
> The weeping birch, the great majestic oak,
> Where dark green ivy forms a winter's cloak;
> The purple heath, where dappled moor cocks crow;
> The sylvan vales, with limping hares below.
> The brooding pheasant, beauty of the wood,
> And spotted trouts that cleave the amber flood.
> For finer walks, for more sequestered bowers,
> For cooler grottoes and for richer flowers,
> For streams that wind more beautiful along,
> For birds with louder chorus to their song,
> For all that gen'rous nature can bestow,
> All Yorkshire scenes to Bingley Vale must bow."

Extensive stone beds of excellent quality are found in the adjoining hills, and are largely worked; but the staple industry of the district is the manufacture of worsted dress goods for the Bradford market. The inhabitants are generally industrious and public-spirited; and the flourishing Co-operative and Building Societies testify to the thriftiness of the population. The educational institutions include denominational Day and Sunday Schools, large Board School, a well-endowed and ably-conducted Grammar School for boys, Mechanics' Institute, with Library and Reading-Room, and Science and Art classes. Religiously the town is well provided for. There are two Churches of the Establishment, an Independent Chapel, fine new Baptist and Wesleyan, with Primitive Methodist and Christian Brethren Chapels, and a Roman Catholic place of worship.

Primitive Methodism was introduced into Bingley in the year 1825. The infancy of the church was feeble, and the difficulties and persecutions of its early history considerable; but for some years it has occupied a position of strength and respectability. Its commodious chapel is occupied by a harmonious, energetic, and generous congregation; and its spacious school and class-rooms are used for the religious instruction of about 500 Sunday scholars.

Mr. Blackburn was appointed to the Bingley Circuit by the Conference of 1875. He entered on his work there with characteristic ardour, and speedily won for himself a solid reputation as a laborious, self-denying, and devoted minister of the gospel. On July 19th, he wrote: "My ministerial work has commenced in good earnest, and the Lord is blessing me with much peace in it so far. May it continue." He rejoiced exceedingly that now he had the opportunity of spending time and strength uninterruptedly in ministering to the mental and spiritual needs of others. He felt his position to be one of grave responsibility, and on assuming it, exclaimed, "Who is sufficient for these things?" But he regarded it as one offering special facilities for usefulness in a great variety of ways; and he did not forget that "our sufficiency is of God."

When appointed to the Bingley Circuit, it was decided that he should reside at Denholme, a large manufacturing village about five miles distant from the head of the Circuit. This arrangement of assigning the junior minister of a station a place of residence in some locality away from the head is not an unusual one; and perhaps much might be said in support of it. Ordinarily the place thus selected is the second in the Circuit in point of numbers and importance;

and by this arrangement it is thought ministerial labours and influence are distributed over the widest possible area, and utilized to the greatest extent. Previous to Mr. Blackburn's appointment to Bingley, that Circuit had been served by one minister only; and when it was decided to apply for another, Denholme Clough, the second place in the Circuit in numbers and strength, naturally desired that he might reside among them. It was decided, however, that Denholme— about a mile nearer Bingley, and more centrally situated for the other places of the Circuit than Denholme Clough— should be his place of residence.

His position here was somewhat peculiar, inasmuch as there was no established congregation of Primitive Methodists in the village. Preaching services had been occasionally held there, and not a few sinners converted, but no permanent cause had been secured. A few of the members of the society at Denholme Clough resided at Denholme; and it was hoped that not only would it be a conveniently situated place of residence for Mr. Blackburn in working the circuit, but that his presence and labours might result in the founding and building up of a Primitive Methodist Church and congregation there. His work was thus largely that of a Home Missionary; and, while taking his full share of preaching appointments through the Circuit, he gave special spiritual oversight, to what might be termed his own "diocese," Denholme and Denholme Clough. His zeal, affability, manliness, and genuine Christian character, soon won for him many friends; and after three years' earnest toil, he left for another and widely different sphere of labour, with the confidence, esteem, and affection of all religious communities, and of the inhabitants in general.

For some time our departed friend had been the subject of an intense longing for purity of heart. In the letter to a young friend, already quoted, he adverts to this theme; and shortly after his entrance on the ministry, his "hunger and thirst" were satisfied. Special revival services were being conducted at Bingley by the Rev. George Warner, Connexional Evangelist. Mr. Blackburn attended, and assisted at, some of these services. They were marked by considerable power, and during the course, a striking incident occurred, which shall be narrated in Mr. Warner's own words:—

"It was on the morning of Sept. 6th, 1875, that the late Rev. R. S. Blackburn called on me at Mr. Crabtree's, and asked if I would like to go out for a walk, saying he would be pleased to show me the neighbourhood. I was settling down to do something I had on hand, but as it was Monday morning, and I was feeling the effects of the exertion of the past day, I thought that the open air might be the best place for me; and at the same time there came an impression, 'perhaps, while he is showing me the neighbourhood, he wants me to shew him something.' So I said I would accept his kindness, and we were soon out of the house.

"'Is there any particular place you would like to see?' he asked. 'We were talking this morning at breakfast about some place called "Druid's Altar," I think I would like to see that.' 'I was thinking of taking you there, but it is some considerable distance, perhaps about two miles.' 'Well, we can walk that, let us go.' We were not very far along the road before he asked, with evident personal interest, 'What are the conditions of a clean heart?' Oh! thought I, then I am right, am I, he wants me to shew him something! So I said, 'One imperative condition is, there must be hunger and thirst for it.' And, 'what are hunger and thirst?' These strong desires for the aliment necessary for the sustenance of our physical frame, as they become ruling passions, and mean supply or death, were explained and illustrated in their application to the mind, in its intense longing for purity of heart. After some thought and consideration he said, very decidedly, 'I am hungering and thirsting for a clean heart.' 'Then God will as certainly give it you as you believe for that specific thing.' As we walked along, he stated some difficulties and objections common in such cases. These we were enabled to remove, and the subject was the absorbing topic of conversation till we reached what is called 'Druid's Altar.'

"On this mass of rock we stood and continued our conversation. I conceived that he desired we should pray, but I thought he may possibly put some confidence in his own prayers, or in mine, so, for awhile I did not propose prayer, for I wanted him to rest his soul fully on Christ for the thing he desired. As we stood on that rock I spoke of its safety as a resting place,—how we were not afraid it would give way beneath us, neither would we though a thousand times our weight were upon it. To this he assented; and then, taking it for a text, God's promises were eternal, immoveable rocks, and to realize their strength and blessedness, we must trust our whole being and destiny to them, as we did our body to that rock. Promise after promise was quoted, and I preached with all my might to that solitary individual in that solitary neighbourhood. This continued, till he said, as his whole frame quivered with emotion, 'I do believe—God does now cleanse my heart!' I said, 'I think we may now praise and pray awhile;' and, kneeling down on the 'Druid's Altar,' we poured out our hearts in praise and petition, and found a very heaven around and within us. We continued in these exercises for some considerable time, and as we prayed, round and round, responding to each other's petitions, faith rose, and our souls were abundantly blest and strengthened. We were not afraid to give expression to our gladness, and there were no religious formalists looking on, or probably their sense of decorum might have been outraged. Unquestionably, the inhabitants of that rock did so shout, that anyone in the vale below might have heard their expressions of gladness.

"As we rose from our knees we found ourselves locked in each other's arms, and among the first things he uttered, he said :—' While we have been here the sun has drunk up the mist out of the valley, and, thank God, the Sun of Righteousness has banished all the mist from my mind, and I am His —wholly His.' Whether the Druids ever worshipped there, I should think questionable, but that by an intelligent act of consecrating faith our dear brother laid his all upon God's altar, there could, I am sure, be no doubt at all. At the public service in the evening he related what took place in the morning on 'Druid's Altar,' and several came forward to the altar of prayer seeking like blessing. I heard afterwards of great power and blessing attending his labours as a consequence, and I hoped that he might have a long lifetime in soul-saving effort. He seemed, physically, mentally, and spiritually adapted to do great things for God; but he is permitted early to rest from his labours, yet, not before he has sown seed, the harvest of which shall follow him.

"When, as one by one the labourers are removed, there is

the more for those left in the field to do, and to do it we must have the 'cleansing' our brother received. It is when we are purged from all uncleanness that 'we are vessels unto honour, sanctified and meet for the Master's use, and prepared unto every good work.' Then, with repeated baptisms of power to meet the responsibilities of our position, and give life and energy to our services, we shall accomplish something for God, and, whether we fall in the high places of the field as did he, or amid the soothing sympathies and sighs of loved ones at home, we may leave to God's choice; He will take care of our souls and of our bone-dust too, and the sowers and reapers shall all rejoice together in the great 'harvest home' by and bye. May the baptism of the Holy Ghost and of fire come upon the labourers, young and old, and may the church be sanctified and the world saved!"

Mr. Blackburn's letters bear ample testimony to the reality and power of the visitation above referred to. Under date of Sept. 15th, 1875, he writes to a friend:—

"Bless the Lord for His goodness. My heart is full; my cup runneth over. Christ is the strength of my soul, and my portion for ever. Oh, is it not sweet to live under the fountain, and to realise its cleansing waters constantly flowing through our hearts, keeping us free from all spiritual disease; how much easier it is to do spiritual work with a healthy soul, than with one diseased by sin. May we always sit at the foot of the cross, and drink of the water of life found there!

"Last Monday morning was a blessed time; but not more so than now. Then I determined to trust the Lord, and He spoke peace to my soul; now, I simply do the same, and He is faithful, and renews His covenant with me. Dark seasons may come, but we must trust Him in darkness. Satan is sure to try us, but Christ is our defence.

"Our Quarterly Meeting was very peaceable; we report 28 increase in members, and I have drawn my first salary—twenty shillings per week—so feel quite wealthy."

Early in his ministerial career, Mr. Blackburn joined the "Christian Workers' Band"—a society comprising believers on Christ of every name, and aiming by the circulation of healthy literature on the subject, and other means, at the promotion of a higher religious life in the churches. As a member of this "Band," he signed the following "Christian Workers' Covenant"—as an expression of his consecration and faith.

"In the strength of the Lord."

1. I consecrate myself unreservedly to Him who has redeemed me, that at all times He may appoint me my place and work ; and that, attentive to the whispers of His grace, I may promptly and cheerfully obey Him.—Rom. xii. 1 ; Psalm cxvi. 16 ; 1 Sam. iii. 10 ; John xv. 16 ; Psalm xxxii. 8, 9 ; Nums. xiv. 24.
2. Trusting in Jesus as my perfect Saviour, I will expect the more abundant life of love, the fulness of the Spirit, the power from on high, which will enable me courageously, tenderly, and wisely, to win souls.—John x. 10 ; Eph. v. 18 ; 2 Tim. i. 7 ; Acts iv. 13 ; 2 Tim. ii. 21 ; Acts xi. 24.
3. I will be a witness unto Jesus : viz. that His Word is true, His atoning sacrifice and intercession availing for all that believe, and His commandments not grievous—that "mighty to save" all who come to Him, He "of God is made unto us wisdom, and righteousness, and sanctification, and redemption."—Acts i. 8 ; Colos. i. 28 ; 1 Cor. i. 30.
4. I will frequently "wait upon the Lord," in the exercise of receptive faith, that my strength may be renewed, and that my spiritual nature may be kept full to overflowing.—Isaiah xl. 30, 31 ; Psalm v. 3 ; Daniel vi. 10 ; John vii. 37, 38 ; Philippians i. 9—11.
5. Resting on the promise, My Word shall not return unto me void, I will daily search the Scriptures, and meditate therein, that the Word of Christ may dwell in me "richly, in all wisdom."—Isaiah lv. 11 ; Joshua i. 8 ; Colos. iii. 16 ; Psalm cxxvi. 6 ; cxix. 97.

6. I will "watch for souls," that as I have opportunity I may either speak, or write, to some one concerning Jesus and His love; and fervently and believingly pray for his salvation.—James v. 16, 19, 20; Daniel xii. 3; Eccles xi. 6.
7. I will endeavour to impress on all those whom the Lord enables me to bring to Jesus, that it is their duty and privilege, in like manner, to be "workers together with Him.—Mark v. 19, 20; Rev. xxii. 17; Psalms xl. 3; Isaiah lxii. 6, 7.

How well this covenant was honoured, it is hoped these pages will, in some measure, testify.

About this time, a gracious quickening in the spiritual life and activities of the society at Denholme Clough occurred, promoted, in some measure, by the fervent spirit and plodding energy of its resident minister. Zeal is often contagious; even icebergs melt in the presence of fire; and sometimes cold religious formalists in the pew, are warmed into sympathy, aspiration and effort, by a "burning and shining light" in the pulpit. The quickened life of the society speedily resulted in more vigorous and fruitful efforts to secure the conversion of sinners. Special revival services were appointed, and the writer distinctly remembers conducting the earlier portion of them, noting the increased "power" that attended them, and meditating with thankfulness and hope on the first fruits of the gathered harvest. A considerable number of souls were converted at these services. Many of them resided in surrounding villages, and joined churches in their own locality; but the nett gain to Denholme Clough Society was about forty members.

Mr. Blackburn's efforts at this time were most assiduous, as the entries in his journal prove:—

Oct. 26th, 1875.—"Went to Harecroft, visited a number of sick people, led the class, and renewed the quarterly tickets."

Oct. 27th.—"Missioned Denholme Clough with tracts, &c., and preached at revival services; had a good congregation and prayer meeting."

Oct. 28th.—"Preached at Denholme Clough; again had a crowded school-room, and a number of sinhers were converted."

Oct. 29th.—"Missioned Denholme Clough; sang up the road to the chapel, and conducted prayer meeting. Several more were converted to-night."

Oct. 31st., Sunday.—"Morning, taught a class, and addressed the Sunday School; afternoon, preached at Denholme Clough; missioned the village between the services; and in the evening conducted the love-feast and prayer meeting. Three were converted."

Nov. 1.—"Walked to East Morton, missioned the village and preached. Not much life in the meeting."

Nov. 2nd.—"Visited nearly every house in East Morton to-day, and missioned the streets, but with very little result."

Nov. 5th.—"Preached at Denholme Clough. The Lord was in our midst, and poured His Spirit upon us. Five persons were brought to the Lord."

Nov. 8th.—"Walked from Bingley to Denholme Clough, visited and sang through a good portion of the village, and preached; several were converted."

Nov. 9th.—"The friends sang in procession through the streets again, and I preached to a rather smaller congregation; a snow-storm having kept many away."

Nov. 10th.—"Visited a large number of families, and

preached to a numerous congregation, and had a prayer meeting afterwards."

Nov. 11th.—"Have had a hard day. Preached at Denholme Clough; many rough men were present, and several were converted."

Nov. 12th.—"At Denholme Clough, formed a Young Men's Improvement Class, read an essay to them, and held a prayer meeting afterwards."

Nov. 19th.—"Poorly in bed all the morning; but after tea joined the procession in singing through the streets, and preached. Several were converted."

Nov. 20th.—"Attended Band Meeting in the evening; and best of all, God was with us. Several persons signified their intention to unite with our society in church fellowship."

Dec. 1st.—"Walked to R——; visited all the houses in the village, preached in the chapel, led the class, and renewed the quarterly tickets. Lord, stir up the sleepy souls!"

Dec. 31.—"Another year has gone. I mourn its shortcomings and sins; am thankful for its blessings, and resolve by God's help to improve on the past. Oh, for purity of motive and divine power!"

For the aggressive work of the Primitive Methodist ministry, Mr. Blackburn had exceptional qualifications. His robust frame, frank and open countenance, manly bearing, and excellent voice; his power of adapting himself to his hearers; his unmistakable earnestness in Christian work, coupled with a singularly kind and sympathetic nature; his enthusiasm for open-air preaching, house to house visitation, and tract distribution; his open-handed generosity, and constant activity in doing good; with the ardour and plodding energy with which he pursued any object on which his heart was set, combined to make him a more than ordinarily efficient agent in aggressive evangelistic work.

During the autumn of 1876, at a meeting of the Ministerial Association of the Leeds District, it was recommended that ministers of contiguous Circuits should assist each other at the "Special Mission Services" during the winter months. In pursuance of this arrangement, Mr. Blackburn held a week's services at Lane Ends, in Keighley 2nd Circuit; and the Rev. J. Ayrton—the present minister of that Circuit—sends the following testimony in regard to these services:—

"I find that our Lane Ends Society have quite vivid recollections of Mr. Blackburn's labours at their Chapel in the winter of 1876-7, according to an arrangement of exchange with my predecessor. The occasion was a week's Special Services. The friends state that he was very assiduous in seeking to promote the work, that he visited, they believe, every house in the neighbourhood (including the *public house*), and some of them several times; and that, for the benefit of the work-people, he conducted, during the dinner hour, short preaching services in Messrs. Haggas's mill yard.

"I may add that when carrying out a similar arrangement of exchange, I conducted a week's services at Denholme Clough Chapel in Nov., 1876, he arranged that he and I should visit separately the people at their homes, he taking one part of the neighbourhood and I another, *in order that we might visit a larger number* than we should have done if we had gone in company. On that occasion he courageously entered a *public house* and kindly invited those present to the services, at the same time handing round a number of the Stirling Tracts, with an ample supply of which he always appeared to be provided. A fortnight afterwards he fulfilled his part of the exchange by conducting Special Services in the Halifax Second Circuit, where I was then stationed; and he adhered to the same plan of *visiting separately*, that we might visit the greater number."

Let it not be supposed, however, that Mr. Blackburn's exemplary diligence in the practical work of the ministry was at the expense of his own mental culture. The curriculum of study demanded by Connexional authorities of all probationers in the Primitive Methodist ministry necessitates hard and constant mental toil; and the position he secured on the Examination Lists, year by year, proves his diligent attention to intellectual training. Ready, as he ever was, to respond to all the calls of practical philanthropy, and usually devoting the afternoon and evening of each day to this work, his mornings were ordinarily spent in the close and consecutive study of the standard works prescribed by Connexional law.

It would probably be impossible to formulate a law that would bear equitably on all ministers, as to the proportion of time which should be devoted to work in the study, and work among the people, respectively. The circumstances of each class of ministers—Methodist, Episcopalian, or Congregational—vary so much that each class must be left to determine that matter for itself; though it may be by no means easy to decide the exact amount of attention to be given to the call for an intelligent ministry on the one hand, and the equally urgent call for a ministry, plodding and energetic in pastoral visitation, Sunday School work, and evening classes on the other. There can be no doubt that

Mr. Blackburn's eminently practical mind led him to assign great prominence in his own ministerial life to work *among* the people. His views on this matter may be gathered from the following selections from his correspondence. To a friend he writes:—

"Your views and mine about mental culture accord in the main. I certainly long to do the most real good work for man's well-being that it is possible to crowd into my short life. We seem to have scholars, writers, preachers, &c., in abundance, while the practical work of visiting the 'fatherless and the widow' is at a discount.

"Preparation for the future is desirable, but is not one's whole life such a preparation? The minor affairs of the circuit, as classes, &c., should not be neglected. Attend to minor matters, more particularly if you are to form a good character. But evening classes, &c., are not minor matters. Attention to the young is the most important work of the ministry. Whilst instructing them I reap a great deal of knowledge. Preparing for the classes is very helpful to me.

"As I have sacrificed college life and taken upon myself the duties of full ministerial life, I dare not neglect the interests of my circuit, however small those interests are, for my own selfish advancement. I can assure you it is a difficult matter to decide where one's duty ends in this. Life is uncertain. Men are perishing. Mental culture, though important, is inferior to heart culture. Whilst gathering crumbs to feed the former, I should like to eat largely of the bread of life. While improving men's external condition, I long to save their souls.

"There is nothing like *contact with* the people for fitting you to deal with them spiritually. Book knowledge, though good, is inferior to practical knowledge."

The entries in Mr. Blackburn's diary during his ministry in the Bingley circuit, are somewhat bare, as compared with the fulness with which he wrote during the periods before and after. They are very largely a record of work in and out of the study; and as such admit of only sparing quotation. A minister's life may often for a long period be a uniformity. Each week brings its work with unvarying regularity; such as the course of study or reading to be pursued; the sermons to be prepared; the journeys into the country to be made for the week-evening services; the classes to be attended; the members to be visited, especially the sick and the sorrowful; and all the other details embraced in the Apostolic phrase "the care of the churches." But this very uniformity may be a virtue, and may tell of the zeal, regularity, and faithfulness with which each week's opportunities for usefulness are improved, and its course of duty observed.

A few more selections are given, taken almost promiscuously, as examples of the daily records of his journal during these years.

Jan. 1st, 1876.—" My hope is that this year will not be made up of resolution only, but of real work done for God. Sermonizing and visiting during the day."

Jan. 10th.—" Visited a great number of people at Harecroft, sang through the streets, and commenced a series of special services."

Jan. 18th.—" Visited and preached at Ryecroft. There must be something wrong in my life, it is so fruitless."

Jan. 20th.—" I am very much dissatisfied with myself. I am not so near to God, and do not realize His presence in my work as I should like. Oh, for the baptism of fire."

March 28th.—" In my study all day, preparing for the Annual Examination."

April 27th.—" Attended one of the classes, and then sat up all night with M. R———, who is ill."

April 28th.—" Spent the day in my study, until 7 o'clock, and then went to the Bible Class."

May 16th.—" Finished reading Macaulay's History; am very much pleased with it, and regret that it goes no further."

June 20th.—" Wrote a sermon; preached at Denholme Clough, and was delighted to hear of additions to the Church."

June 29th.—" Reading all day. My life seems fruitless."

Aug. 13th.—" Preached at Bingley morning and night, and Ryecroft in the afternoon. Visited several sick persons, and was much blest in my work."

Aug. 27th.—" In the morning gave a School address, and preached afternoon and evening. It being Bingley Tide, there was a smaller attendance at the services. Feasts have not one redeeming feature."

Nov. 30th.—" Studying Homiletics, Logic, and History, all day."

Dec. 2nd.—" Sermonizing in the morning; tract distributing in the afternoon; reading at night."

Dec. 6th.—" Preached at Wilsden in the evening, and then sat up all night with Mr. A. Philips, who is on his death-bed."

Dec. 28th.—" Studying Butler's Analogy; preparing sermon and letter writing."

Dec. 31st.—" This year has been very varied in its experiences; it opened with fair prospects, it closes with many disappointments. My christian life is not what I could wish; yet my trust is in the Saviour, who will pardon the past, and give me help for the future."

Jan. 3rd, 1877.—" In returning from my appointment to-night a deep fall of snow made the journey very laborious."

March 25th.—" Morning, gave School address at Wilsden, preached there in the afternoon, and at Bingley at night. Good services, and one man converted."

May 11th.—" Reading Theology and preparing for the pulpit."

May 21st.—" Went for a two days' trip to Edinburgh, had a pleasant but toilsome day at sightseeing; visited Leith, Portobello, Newhaven, &c."

May 22nd.—" Visited Stirling, Callander, &c. Left Edinburgh at 10.30 p.m. for Bingley."

June 21st.—" Morning, in my study; afternoon, visiting; and evening, preached in the open-air."

Aug. 11th.—Morning, in the study; afternoon, distributing tracts; evening, at the Young Men's Class.

Sept. 2nd.—" Morning (Sunday), taught select class, and gave a school address; afternoon, taught the class again and then preached; had open-air service, and then preached in the evening."

Oct. 22nd.—" Very poorly to-day. Afternoon, visited, distributed tracts, and wrote letters; in the evening preached in a cottage, and there was one convert. Led class afterwards—a good time."

Dec. 19th.—" Morning, in my study; afternoon, attended

a Mothers' Meeting, and gave a Bible lesson; baptized several children in the evening."

Dec. 31st.—" This year has been characterised by hard work. I am earnestly yearning for more devotedness to God."

Mr. Blackburn had a profound admiration for the beauties of nature, and a strong wish to see what was going on in the world. During his early manhood he was accustomed to employ his holiday in the summer or autumn in taking extensive walking tours. On one occasion the Midland and Western Counties of England were the scene of his pedestrian excursions; and there are few places of interest in those regions he did not visit and inspect. On another occasion he explored the hills and dales of the North of Yorkshire; while a third year found him traversing the Counties on the South Coast, and walking for many miles along the shores washed by the waters of the English Channel. At another time he crossed the Straits of Dover, and spent some time in France, principally in Paris and its surroundings; and Scotland was more than once the scene of a pleasurable tour. The copious notes made on these occasions lie before us as we write, and evince no small amount of historical, geographical, and antiquarian information. The notes of one of his excursions in Scotland were afterwards expanded into a lecture for the benefit of his Young Men's Class; and judging from its animated descriptions, historic facts, and personal allusions, it must have been both interesting and instructive.

Under the genial influences of reciprocated friendship, and fervent Christian love, his social nature developed and exhibited some of the noblest graces of the Spirit. The following selections from letters written to a friend, who was passing through a keen trial and painful bereavement, by the sickness and death of a relative, will illustrate his deeply sympathetic spirit, and simple, child-like trust in the wisdom, power, and love of God.

"*Feb.* 12*th*, 1877.

"MY DEAR ——

"It may be well sometimes to face the troubles of the future, as they cast their shadows before them ; but I question the wisdom of anticipating them frequently and protractedly. God will prepare your way before you, helping you to surmount the difficulties as you come at them, and will give you the desire of your heart by granting His continued presence. 'I will never leave thee nor forsake thee.' Our earthly friends are taken, one by one. They leave earth for heaven. There they await our joining them, increasing the attractions of the better world, and causing earth to lose its charms. When they are almost all gone, our turn comes. But amidst all, the Father remains with us, to console, guard, sustain, and conduct us on our journey, often permitting us to see, by faith, the heavenly land, and assuring us of the re-union above. 'Bless the Lord, O my soul, and all that is within me, bless His holy name.' He is a satisfying portion."

"*May* 28*th*, 1877.

"MY DEAR ——

"Your leaning upon God, in the darkness of the last fortnight, will do you good. 'All things work together for good, to them that love God.' Child-like confidence pleases our Father. He requires it from His children. We have the lesson to learn in different ways. I do not think that your mother's sufferings are brought upon her solely to teach us this and other lessons ; but these are some of the good things working out of her sufferings.

"It is difficult in these times of perplexity and painful excitement, to calmly leave circumstances in the Lord's hands ; and yet how wise, when we are helplessly battling with the foe, to look up into the face of our divine Captain for orders, and calmly await his commands.

patience, and resignation to His will, possess your soul! The cup of divine consolation is held to your lips; drink deeply of it. The same Saviour who wept with Mary and Martha is with you, and offers you His sympathy; take it, and apply it to the wounds of your heart."

"*Aug.* 28*th*, 1877.

"MY DEAR ——

"I can understand, to a certain degree, your feelings while you are watching by the side of the sick one; and I can assure you this experience will bear fruit in the future. What you require for the present, is a strong confidence in our Father, who does all things well. He will be with you. Do not infer from this that I think you lack faith in Him. I believe you do trust Him, or you would have given way under the burden long since. Jesus is your stay! Don't anticipate events. Take each moment with its experience; and with your mind stayed on God, you will be kept in 'perfect peace.'

"Jesus says, 'I have prayed for thee, that thy faith fail not.' Oh, how delightful is this assurance! Jesus is watching by your side, knowing your heart-pangs, administering sympathy, and inviting the weary and heavy laden to come to Him for rest, perfect rest."

"*Sept.* 18*th*, 1877.

"MY DEAR ——

"Accept my sympathy and assurances of prayer on your behalf this morning. The solemn news you send me is not altogether unexpected, though it is difficult to realize. I trust you may be upborne. Our Father's goodness will appear in some special way in all this trial. The Lord will hide you in the hollow of His hand, shield you beneath His wing, bear you in His everlasting arms, be your refuge, and strength, and present help, in time of trouble. 'Be still, and know that I am God,' is His word. May you have perfect trust, that you may have perfect peace."

"*Oct.* 8*th*, 1877.

"MY DEAR ——

"I do pray that your faith may not fail, and that the weight pressing upon you may soon be lifted away. Let us meet at the mercy-seat, and there obtain 'grace to help in time of need.' 'Unto the upright there ariseth light in the darkness.' 'Then they cried unto the Lord in their trouble, and He delivered them out of their distresses. And He led them forth by the right way, that they might go to a city of habitation.' 'Truly God is good to Israel, even to such as are of a clean heart.' I have just been reading in the Psalms. What food there is in them for the sorrowing! Take to yourself their promises of strength. This morning I visited a young woman dying of consumption. She is only 29 years of age, and has a husband who believes there is no hereafter. She is often troubled with doubts as to whether she is truly converted or not; and, oh, how earnestly she prayed!"

"*Oct.* 15*th*, 1877.

"My Dear ——

"The sufferings of your precious mother cannot be forgotten— they are indelibly written on your memory and heart; but may they not be comparatively lost in the rest and peace she is now enjoying! Remember, that they 'are not worthy to be compared with the glory that shall be revealed in her.' They have worked out for her 'a far more exceeding and eternal weight of glory.' Oh! to be at rest, and with Jesus, must be glorious! She no longer needs our sympathy.

"Last Tuesday I visited a woman who has had several 'strokes,' which have bereft her of the power of speech, and the use of one of her limbs. She is entirely dependent on an allowance from the 'parish, and what friends give her; but Jesus is with her and her life is full of sunshine.

"Yesterday I visited the wife of a manufacturer, surrounded by all the comforts this life can give. Christ is with her in her affliction; she told me she was 'fully prepared.' Our Saviour goes to the deepest depths of poverty, and to the wealthiest of earth's sons and daughters; and wherever He treads there is light and blessedness.

"''Peace I leave with you, My peace I give unto you; not as the world giveth, give I unto you. Let not your heart be troubled, neither let it be afraid.' Open your heart, and the Saviour will pour into it the balm of His love and peace; that alone can heal the wound."

"*Oct.* 29*th*, 1877.

"My Dear ——
   " ———. Last week I saw another life ebbing out; and though accompanied by much suffering, it was a triumphant closing scene. Jesus was present, shining on the face of the sufferer. She said, 'He is with me in the valley.' I have witnessed several conversions lately. It is a glorious thing to live to win sinners to Jesus, and to build characters for heaven. Oh, for a deeper devotedness to this work!"

The annexed paper was read to the Sunday School Teachers of the Bingley Circuit, at a quarterly meeting of the Station Union. It explains itself; and though somewhat hastily prepared, its strong common sense will, we think, commend it to the judgment of those interested in the work of Sunday Schools :—

THE QUALIFICATIONS OF A SUNDAY SCHOOL SUPERINTENDENT.

It is with considerable diffidence I enter upon the work of laying before you a few thoughts for discussion upon the important subject which heads this paper. First, because of the short time afforded for its preparation, as I only received Bro. Crabtree's note yesterday, informing me of his unavoidable absence, and requesting me to supply his place this afternoon. Secondly, because of my lack of practical knowlege of the subject. I suppose, as there are some here to-day who have held the office of superintendent for many years, and have thus gained an experimental knowledge of its work, and the necessary qualifications for it, that they are much better fitted to write an essay on this topic than I. However, we shall probably have the benefit of their views in the discussion following, and so shall not be great losers.

I think that, perhaps, I should have found it easier to have written a paper on "The necessary qualifications of an Essay Writer;" but that would not have met the wants of a Teachers' Conference. So, here I am, and here is my paper.

I do not make these remarks to prevent severe criticism, for that would defeat the object of the meeting, as I understand we are met for mutual benefit; but as an explanation of defectiveness, which I am conscious will be patent to you when you hear it read.

This subject has been chosen with some objects in view; and I presume these objects are :—(1) To guide us in the choice of suitable superintendents; (2) to urge those who are in the superintendency to seek improvement; and (3) to induce those who may be superintendents at some future time, to fit themselves for the work of the office.

(1) In our choice of superintendents we need to be *discreet* and *practical*. Sentimentality has guided us too much in the past. One teacher says, "Mr. Smith is an old teacher, and has never had the office; let us make him superintendent for next year." Another says, "Mr. Jones has worked hard for the school many years; he ought to be honoured; we will elect him to the superintendency."

Now I fail to see that age is the *only* qualification for a superintendent. I certainly think that all other things being equal, we ought to choose the oldest, but not when he is deficient in every other respect.

Nor do I think that the office should be conferred upon a man *merely* as an honour, if he be not qualified. If you want to honour an earnest worker, give him a gold medal, a five pound note, or pension him; and then elect your superintendent from among the more efficient members of your Teachers' Meeting.

A good business man, wanting an overlooker, will choose the man according to his own judgment best adapted for the work. He would be considered very foolish if he went to a worn-out weaver—though the old man might have served him very faithfully, and for a great length of time—and exalted him to the vacant position. But no good business man would ever think of such a thing. If he wished to repay the man's faithfulness, he would make him a handsome present, or pension him off.

A political party wanting a *Leader* would not think a faithful adherence to its principles for forty or fifty years sufficient qualification for the position, unless there was leading ability coupled with it. No. They would try to secure the ablest man, and reward the other with a peerage. Much more should we be governed by wisdom in the choice of superintendents.

(2) Many already in the superintendency are not so *efficient* as they might be. What shall they do? Give up the office? No! But perhaps on hearing the qualifications they will say, "We can never reach the standard." Probably you cannot, and you never will if you remain as you are; but a failure is far more honourable if we have tried to avert it, than if we had made no attempt to succeed. Aim high, my brother! even if you fail you will get to a higher altitude than if you sit down in despair.

(3) All aspirants for 'the office should be *preparing* themselves for its duties. As the youth who intends to shine in the commercial world, devotes his time and attention to the study of all those things which constitute a man of business; as the young man aspiring after political honours, studies political economy, and constitutional history; so should every one, who has any idea of ever being chosen for the superintendency of a Sabbath School, be seeking a thorough knowledge of its work, and the qualifications necessary to a faithful and efficient discharge of its duties.

To form a correct estimate of the qualifications necessary in a superintendent, we must first acquaint ourselves with his work. On referring to the Conference minutes, I find he is responsible (1) for conducting the services of the school; (2) for the admission and removal of scholars; (3) for the arrangement of classes and teachers; and (4) for the internal management of a school, subject to the directions of the Teachers' Meeting and Committee.

Thus you see he is, (1) the Priest of the school, leading its devotions; (2) the Judge, who has to decide when the behaviour of the scholars calls for expulsion; (3) the General, arranging the forces, and placing suitable officers over the different brigades of the army; and (4) the Manager to conduct the business to the most satisfactory results.

His position therefore is a very onerous one, his work arduous, and the qualifications for such an office are numerous and important.

I. *He should be a man of mental cultivation, and of ready utterance.*

Flagrant grammatical errors, historical or scientific mistakes, are—in these days of advanced education—soon detected by the scholars, and only call forth ridicule from them.

His knowledge should be extensive, not only in matters of ordinary education, but of human nature, so many different dispositions and characters are brought under his jurisdiction, and many of them requiring different modes of treatment.

His knowledge should extend to every branch of Sunday School work. Having an oversight of the whole, he should be acquainted with the details, from the infant to the select classes, from the position of the lowest teacher to that of the librarian and secretary.

II. *He should be a man of administrative ability.* Not despotic, but firm; dealing out justice without partiality. To do this he must have a clear judgment to discern the right, an honest heart to decide for the right, and a firm will to carry out the right.

III. *He should be a man of unimpeachable character, and free from bad habits.* His presence *in* the school should command the respect of all, because of his general bearing *out* of it. Violent tempers are out of place in such a man.

I knew a man who was so violent in school that he would strike the boys on the head with the Bible; which action lowered their opinion of the book, caused them to lose all respect for the man, and secured for him the nick-name of "Cayenne Pepper."

Self-denial should characterise him, and habits of temperance, demanded by the evils associated with the drinking customs of our times; and abstinence from tobacco and snuff. As so many physical and moral calamitous consequences are entailed on youthful life by these things, their disuse by Christian people is loudly called for.

One superintendent I knew got the name of "Snuffy Tommy" among the boys, because of his free use of snuff, both in and out of school.

The superintendent of a school holds a very important position in relation to these pressing questions, and ought to face them honestly.

As the *general* of the large army of Sunday School workers, whose object is to throw down the kingdom of Satan, and build up the kingdom of God; as the *father* of that large family of philanthropists, whose aim is to better the moral condition of the world, he should lead the van in the crusade against all these gigantic evils that are sapping the very foundations of our national, social, and religious life.

IV. *He should be a man of earnestness and diligence.* As a sleepy head will prostrate the body, so a lifeless superintendent will cause death in the school. No duty should be thought too mean for his attention. Integrity should mark all his work.

V. *Above all, he should be a man of deep piety.* Having been to the feet of Jesus, and found pardon himself, he will be able to lead others there. Earnest prayer is indispensable. "They that wait upon the Lord shall renew their strength; they shall mount up with wings as eagles; they shall run, and not be weary; and they shall walk, and not faint."—*Isa.* xl. 31.

He needs divine wisdom. "If any of you lack wisdom, let him ask of God, that giveth to all men liberally and upbraideth not; and it shall be given him."—*James* i. 5.

The spirit of Christian love must fill his soul, shedding its influence around, dispersing the darkness of sin. He must be a tree of righteousness, spreading his branches over the whole school, dropping the fruits of holiness upon the scholars, and filling the air with sweet perfume. He must feed their souls with that heavenly food, of which, if they eat, they shall never hunger. He must be filled with the Holy Ghost—that divine power, without which all our efforts to Christianise the world will be fruitless. Without this "unction from the Holy One," all our intellectualism, all our amiability of disposition and manner, all our governing power, will be vain.

The locomotive engine may be perfect in its mechanism; but is only so much lumber, and is entirely useless without the fire. The sailing vessel may be constructed on the most approved principle; but without the wind, it is no better than a shapeless log. The cannon may be made of highly polished steel, and loaded with the best powder, and most destructive shot; but without the spark it is quite harmless.

But put water into the boiler of the engine, and fire under, and that which was simply a piece of lumber, becomes almost a living thing, and runs off with a village at its back. Fill the sails of that ship with wind, and away she speeds over the ocean, carrying our merchandise to foreign lands, and bringing to us the comforts and luxuries of life. Apply the match to the touch-hole of the cannon, and it at once becomes the most effective weapon of warfare. So the superintendent may have every human qualification for his work, and yet may be as useless as the engine without fire, the vessel without wind, and the cannon without spark.

Christian gravity, coupled with cheerfulness of manner, and kindness of disposition, will win the hearts of the children to *himself*; but his object should be to win them for Christ, and for this he needs divine help.

This aid may very naturally be expected—the nature of the work renders it probable. Christ's solicitude for children makes it certain. "Then were brought to Him little children, that he should put His hands on them, and pray : and the disciples rebuked them. But Jesus said, Suffer little children, and forbid them not, to come unto Me : for of such is the kingdom of heaven. And He laid His hands on them."—*Matt.* xix., 13-15.

Again, when he appeared to His disciples after His resurrection, He said to Peter—"Feed my lambs."

The experience of others confirms this. May every Superintendent of our Sunday Schools be endued with power from on high !

Towards the close of the year 1877, considerable excitement was occasioned in the village of Denholme, by the placing on a tombstone in the Baptist Chapel graveyard a somewhat remarkable inscription. Mr. Blackburn, ever ready to extract from any public event whatever it would contribute to public advantage, made the notable epitaph the subject of a lecture or sermon.

We subjoin his notes of this address. Considerable controversy raged on this theme for some time in the locality ; but having publicly delivered himself on the matter, we do not find that he took any further part in it. Ultimately, the tombstone was laid on its face by the authorities of the Baptist Chapel, and the obnoxious epitaph hidden from view.

A NOTABLE EPITAPH.

"What went before, and what will follow me, I regard as two black impenetrable curtains, which hang down at the two extremities of human life, and which no living man has yet drawn aside. Many hundreds of generations have already stood before them with their torches guessing anxiously what lies behind. On the curtain of futurity, many see their own shadows, the forms of their own passions, enlarged and put in motion; they shrink in terror at this image of themselves. Poets, philosophers, and founders of States, have painted this curtain with their dreams, more smiling or more dark, as the sky above them was cheerful or gloomy, and their pictures deceive the eye when viewed from a distance. Many jugglers too, make profit out of this our universal curiosity. By their strange mummeries they have set the outstretched fancy in amazement. A deep silence reigns behind this curtain; no one once within will answer those he has left without; all you can hear is the hollow echo of your question, as if you shouted in a cavern."*

Logic. A complete argument consisting of two premises and a conclusion, called a syllogism. Holyoake's premises fallacious.

1. Unless some one return to earth from the future life, there is no future life.
2. No one has returned from the future life. Therefore, there is no future life.

The first premise is false. It ignores every kind of evidence but one—that of the senses. It ignores internal consciousness, revelation, and faith. The epitaph speaks of universal curiosity guessing anxiously what is behind the curtains, proving at once that it is an instinct of our being to expect a future life; and if it be instinct, there must be something to satisfy its craving. This internal consciousness is a powerful argument in favour of a future life.

Again, if there be a God, which infidelity does not deny, it is only reasonable to expect that He would reveal Himself to man. How has

---

* Holyoake.—" The Logic of Death."

He done this? By ancient philosophy? No. The epitaph speaks of poets, philosophers, and founders of States, having painted the future with pictures that deceive the eye. A philosopher (according to Ogilvie) is "a person versed in the principles of nature, and morality; one who devotes himself to the study of moral and intellectual science; one who is profoundly versed in any science." One would think that if any man *unassisted* could arrive at a satisfactory conclusion, a philosopher could. But no; Plato, Cicero, Socrates, and others, have failed. The highest attainment of philosophy was to raise "an altar to the UNKNOWN God," telling us nothing of His character, attributes, or the relation He sustains to His creatures.

Has He revealed Himself by jugglery? Certainly not. Many jugglers—who, according to the authority quoted before, are "those who practice or exhibit by sleight of hand; who make sport by tricks of extraordinary dexterity; cheats, deceivers; or trickish fellows"— have used heathenish practices to further their own selfish ends, and gain undue power over the minds of men; but their jugglery has not assisted in enlightening the world on the important question at issue. Then, where are we to look for the revelation? In the Scriptures—the Divine Word. Proofs of its divinity are everywhere manifest.

By the truthfulness of its prophecies. Voltaire boasted that with one hand he would overthrow that edifice of Christianity which required the hands of twelve men to build up. The press which he employed at Ferney for printing his blasphemies, was actually employed afterwards at Geneva in printing the Holy Scriptures. At another time he said that "he was living in the twilight of Christianity;" and so he was; but not the twilight of evening, as he meant, but of the morning.

Paine, on his return from France, sitting in the City Hotel, Broadway, New York, surrounded by many leading men in the city, predicted that "in five years there would not be a Bible in America." Now there are millions. These are specimens of the prophecies of infidelity. The Scripture prophecies do not present such a miserable failure. See the numbers of them that have been fulfilled to the very letter and time, and others that are being fulfilled now.

The writers of Scripture foretold the scattering of the Israelitish nation; and are they not spread over the whole world?

They predicted the rise and fall of the Babylonish, the Persian, the Grecian, and the Roman Empires.

They prophesied the coming of Christ, and the establishment of His blessed kingdom on the earth; and have not all these taken place? The fulfilment of its prophecies stamps with divinity the blessed Bible.

Further, its divinity is proved by the *wisdom of its teachings*, and *its tenacity of life;* for while other systems have fallen, this has risen. While the storms of persecution from infidelity and religious bigotry have battered against the Bible, it has sailed nobly forward over the tempestous sea. Infidelity acknowledges its own weakness; the Bible asserts its own power.

The epitaph speaks of two black impenetrable curtains at the extremities of human life. The Bible lifts these curtains, showing us the origin of human life; "and the Lord God formed man of the dust of the ground, and breathed into his nostrils the breath of life; and man became a living soul."—Gen. ii. 7. Nay, it goes further, and gives us a description of the formation of the world; (Gen. i.) thus telling me "what went before me."

It lifts the curtain of futurity, and shows me what is to come after, and it lays down suitable laws for the government of my life, and for my security. An infidel and a Christian travelling over a barren country, benighted, came across a hut inhabited by an old man and woman and two sons, looking as wild as the country they lived in. The infidel felt uneasy as to his safety till the Bible was read and prayer offered, when his fears fled, and he retired to rest fearing no harm.

It presents a vast number of precious promises to inspire my energies, and inflame my enthusiasm. Two professional men of note, sceptics, were fast friends; one died, but left a will appointing a good Christian man his executor. Infidelity presents very little motive for living; while the Bible teems with incentives to do right.

Again; the epitaph ignores one of the grandest powers of the soul —*faith*. I met with an atheist the other day who made the ridiculous statement that faith was nothing. We should soon find out its value if it were taken from us. Our business, family and national relations are very much dependent on faith. The credit system in business, without which it would be almost impossible to carry on the trade of the country, is largely done upon faith. The closest unions in domestic life are entered into chiefly on faith. Our representatives to any governing body, such as School Boards, Boards of Guardians, Council Boards, and Parliament, are sent in faith. Faith is an instinct of human nature, and always should be allowed to operate when the evidence is sound. Many of us have not been to America, yet we believe there is such a place from the evidence received. Men of sterling character have told us of it. Now what is the evidence in favour of a future life? I will only refer to the character of the witnesses, the grounds of their evidence, and the reward of their toils.

Jesus Christ, the founder of Christianity—speaking of Him as a man —possessed a character that was unimpeachable. Paine, after scandalizing the account of Christ's supernatural birth in his "Age of Reason," uses the following language :—"Nothing that is here said can apply, even with the most distant disrespect, to the moral character of Jesus Christ. He was a virtuous and amiable man. The morality that He preached and practiced was of the most benevolent kind; and though similar systems of morality have been practiced by Confucius, and by some of the Greek philosophers many ages before, and the Quakers since, and by many good men in all ages, it has not been exceeded by any." Again he says, "Christ called men to the practice of moral virtues, and the belief of one God. The great trait in his character is philanthropy." Leguinia, the great French Atheist, says of Jesus Christ, "He called Himself the Son of God, and who among mortals dare say He was not? He always displayed virtue; He always spoke according to the dictates of reason; He always preached up wisdom; He sincerely loved all men, and wished to do good even to His persecutors; He developed all the principles of moral equality, and of the purest patriotism; He met danger undismayed; He described the hard-heartedness of the rich; He attacked the pride of Kings; He dared to resist even in the face of tyrants; He despised glory and fortune; He was sober; He solaced the indigent; He taught the unfortunate how to suffer; He sustained weakness; He fortified decay; He consoled misfortune; He knew how to shed tears with those that wept ; He taught men to subjugate their passions, to think, to reflect, to love one another, and to live happily together ; He was hated by the powerful, whom He offended by His teaching, and persecuted by the wicked, whom He unmasked ; and He died under the indignation of the blind and deceived multitude for whose good He had always lived."

There is no need to enlarge upon these testimonies to the moral character of Christ; coming from the source they do, they are conclusive.

Blemished character damages evidence. Any possibility of interested motives will discredit testimony. What was the reward of Jesus and His followers who taught the doctrines we are contending for? They were hunted from town to town, scourged, ill-treated, and finally martyred. Starving, their gain ; and martyrdom, their price. Such men are worthy of confidence.

Christianity carries its own credentials with it. Its wonderful works, coupled with its nobility of character, its power over the lives of men, its grand achievements in the past, its institutions of philanthropy speak volumes in its favour.

It requires more faith to be an infidel than a Christian, and yet infidelity professes to ignore faith.

Read and comment upon the epitaph.

"Torches."—Human lights are of no use comparatively ; the "Sun of righteousness" alone can disperse the shades of spiritual night. "Guessing anxiously." Infidelity guesses, but Christianity knows by the certainties of faith. "In terror." This applies only to the unbeliever. Hume, the infidel historian, says, "I am affrighted and confounded at that forlorn condition in which I am placed by my philosophy. When I look abroad, I foresee on every side dispute, contradiction, and distraction. When I turn my eye inward I find nothing but doubt and ignorance. Where am I, or what? To what causes do I owe my existence, and to what condition shall I return? I am confounded by these questions, and begin to fancy myself in the most deplorable condition imaginable, environed by the deep darkness." I am neither anxious nor afraid, but at perfect peace, because the revelation of God clears away my doubts. "Viewed from a distance." Very few sceptics come near enough; they almost all view religion from a distance. If you want to know the nature and composition of anything, you must examine it. Get your Bibles and study them with the desire to know the truth, and then you will not so easily be deceived.

"No one within will answer those he has left without." Let us go to the borders and see what answer they give. Voltaire, as he approached death, showed signs of wishing to return to that God whom he had often blasphemed. He both called and wrote for the priest. Many times was he heard crying in plaintive accents, "Oh, Christ! Oh, Jesus Christ!" and then to complain that he was abandoned of God and man. At one time he was discovered by his attendant with a book of prayers in his hand, endeavouring with a faltering tongue to repeat some of the petitions for mercy. He had fallen from his bed in convulsive agonies, and lay on the floor foaming with impotent despair, exclaiming "Will not this God whom I have denied save me too! Cannot infinite mercy extend to me!" All who were in attendance on him declared it was terrible to be in his presence.

Paine, during the last fortnight of his life, dared not to be left alone for a moment, and would repeatedly cry, "Lord, help me; God, help me; Jesus Christ, help me;" in a tone of voice that alarmed all who were in the house.

What a contrast does the death of the Christian present! Stephen: "Lord Jesus, receive my spirit." Paul: "I have fought a good fight, I have finished my course, I have kept the faith: henceforth there is laid up for me a crown of righteousness, which the Lord, the righteous Judge, shall give me at that day; and not to me only, but unto all them also that love his appearing." Wesley: "Pray and praise." "The best of all is God is with us." Mrs. B—— (a lady Mr. B. had visited during her sickness): "It is all right." J—— G—— (a local preacher recently deceased): "And now, that the death dew lies cold on my brow, if ever I loved thee, my Jesus, 'tis now." Dr. Payson: "My God is in this room; I see Him; and oh, how lovely is the sight; how glorious does He appear; worthy of ten thousand hearts, if I had so many to give. The battle's fought, the victory's won! The victory is won for ever! I am going to bathe in an ocean of purity, and benevolence, and happiness for ever."

Now we have presented you with the "despairing wail" of infidelity on the one hand, and the assurance of the faith of the gospel on the other. Darkness, misery, and death; or light, happiness, and eternal life. Which will you choose? The day of death is approaching. "We must all appear before the judgment seat of Christ, to give an account of the deeds done in the body, whether they be good or bad."

"Seek ye the Lord while He may be found; call upon Him while He is near; let the wicked forsake his way, and the unrighteous man his thoughts; and let him return unto the Lord, and He will have mercy upon him; and to our God, for He will abundantly pardon." "Ho, every one that thirsteth, come ye to the waters." "Come unto Me all ye that labour, and are heavy laden, and I will give you rest." "Him that cometh unto Me I will in no wise cast out."

Here is a *rock* to build upon; and if you build thereon, your house shall stand firm, amid the storms of the last day, when the stars shall fall from their courses, and when the universe shall be illuminated by the conflagration of burning worlds.

The following contributions from persons intimately acquainted with Mr. Blackburn's character and work, during his ministry in the Bingley circuit, may further elucidate this part of his career.

An intelligent matron of the Church at Denholme Clough, writes:—

"As regards dear Mr. Blackburn's work here, I scarcely know where to begin. It was the same here as everywhere else, like the blessed Master, he went about doing good to the souls and bodies of those he came in contact with.

"He laboured hard in connection with the services of the sanctuary, and besides his ordinary work, he formed two classes, one for the young men, and the other for the young women; and in this department he did all that lay in his power to teach everything that would be of use to them in their after life. The class for females was given up when he left, but the good that was received through his instrumentality will not soon be forgotten. He did not lose sight of these classes when he was in Africa, mention being made of them in his letters. The first winter he was here he worked very arduously in connection with special services, at which time both young and old were brought to the Saviour, and it ever seemed to be his aim to find something to do for those who had begun to serve the Lord Christ. The result was, that two local preachers and two assistant leaders sprang from the converts. There were several additions to the church after that, and I have heard them speak, in very touching language, of how he pleaded with them, and sought to win them to Jesus. When they could not be won in one way he would try another. His equal has not been known in the neighbourhood for visiting; he would go from house to house with the silent messenger, inviting persons to the House of God, and speaking words of kindness and sympathy to all whom he met at these times. The beer-houses were not passed, and he has been known to kneel down in the midst of a number of men who were drinking, and beseech God to have mercy upon them, and to change their hearts; and tears were seen to trickle down the cheeks of the company, as he thus pleaded for them."

Mr. E. Redman, of Denholme, thus writes:—

"My acquaintance with the late Rev. Richard Stead Blackburn, during the three years that we resided together, with my mother (Mrs. Dixon), was of a very pleasant character.

"I am unable, with my pen, to express the amount of love and esteem in which he was held in this place, not only by our family and the members of his own society, but also by the members and friends of other denominations. At home we found him always kind, obliging, and willing to comply with the requirements of circumstances. I have heard my mother say, that a less selfish man she never met with.

"As a preacher he was very faithful and energetic.

"During the summer months he was to be seen and heard singing through the streets, sometimes with so little assistance that many in his position would have abandoned the idea—

> ' O for a trumpet voice,
> On all the world to call,
> To bid their hearts rejoice
> In Him who died for all.
> For all my Lord was crucified,
> For all, for all, my Saviour died.'

And at some convenient place he would make a stand and conduct an open-air service, and faithfully exhort sinners to flee from the wrath to come.

"As a visitor, he excelled any minister I have known, and in this capacity he gained the esteem of a great many families outside his own Connexion. After exhorting and praying with the sick, his benevolent heart would not let him retire without contributing to their temporal wants, and he often made the widow's heart rejoice. He was a thorough going total abstainer. The Temperance and Alliance movements received his earnest attention, as far as his time would allow.

"In politics he was a faithful Liberal.

"Last, but not least, his piety exhibited itself in more than words; it breathed in his spirit and lived in his life. As a son and brother he adorned the doctrine of God his Saviour. We were sorry when he nobly decided to leave his native land to labour on such a dangerous island as Fernando Po, but it was like him to do so; nothing seemed too much for him to do in the cause of Christ. Little did we think that his Master was so soon going to take him to Himself.

"The unexpected news of his death was received in this village with deep and sincere lamentation. But what a grand consolation to the dear ones he has left behind that he has gone to be with Jesus, which is far better. Let us all

> 'Rejoice for a brother deceased,
>   Our loss is his infinite gain,
> A soul out of prison released,
>   And freed from its bodily chain;
> With songs let us follow his flight,
>   And mount with his spirit above,
> Escaped to the mansions of light,
>   And lodged in the Eden of love.'"

The following contributions have also come to hand from two friends residing at Denholme and Denholme Clough. The first is from Denholme, voluntarily sent by a person unknown to the writer.

"It is with the ardent wish of stimulating others to strive after things which are beautiful and excellent that I write you a few lines to the memory of one much beloved.

"The first time that I saw Mr. Blackburn, and heard him speak, was when he was engaged in open-air preaching.

Standing upon a few stones piled one upon another, he told to passers by 'the old, old story of Jesus and his love.' It may be truly said of him, that copying the example of his Divine Master, 'he went about doing good.' With unabated zeal he preached the gospel, and many know how every selfish feeling was absorbed and lost in him in the wish to do good. How could such a one be other than devout and useful? Most generous and self-denying, he sought not his own ease and gain, but souls—souls for his Master. He was especially rich in sympathy, which he poured without stint into the wounded hearts of the sorrowful. He was ever ready to listen to the tale of sorrow or of joy. He did not look indifferently off when you spoke to him, as if he had some other business to attend to. He was always receptive and kind, and had, I believe, a sincere desire to help. His consecration to his Divine Master and His Master's work was complete."

The second one is from Denholme Clough.

"I well remember in the first year Mr. Blackburn was with us, having four months' sickness, and during that time having much of his visiting and sympathy. I owe a debt of love I cannot pay, but pray that the work may be made a blessing. One night he called, and said he had helped a drunken woman up from Denholme, out of the way of the police. He visited her afterwards, and was made the means, in God's hands, of leading her to Jesus. Once, while visiting he was so wet with the rain, that the water ran off his clothes on the floor, and he said there was not a house in Denholme Clough that night, but had had a tract and a word of invitation; and this was often the case during his ministry here. In all sorts of weather he would sing up the road. An old man more than seventy years of age says, that 'never a man came like him.'

"One evening he preached near to a public-house, and some men brought a quart of beer to him, and asked him to drink; but he looked at it smilingly, and said, 'Thank you; I don't take that sort of stuff;' and they drank the beer while we sung and he preached with his usual zeal from the text, 'Wherefore do ye spend money for that which is not bread?' One of the men who drank the beer was seized with a fever soon after and died, the sermon being to him the last offer of mercy. One night Mr. B. told me he was not well, and I said to him, 'if you don't take better care of yourself, you won't be in the ministry long;' to which he replied, 'I had rather die at thirty years of age, having done all I could for Jesus, than live to be seventy, and be an idler in the cause.'"

The next testimony is from Miss Adams, a pious and intelligent young lady, then one of the members at Denholme, and who played the harmonium at the public services :—

"As you will know, Mr. Blackburn's work at Denholme was much the same one week as another, but I do not think anyone but God knew how earnestly and zealously he did that work—visiting families of any denomination as well as those who belonged to none, and by earnest invitations, trying to bring them to the Master; or if they were Christians, to encourage them on their way. Often to the sick have I known him go, taking physical comforts and necessaries, as well as spiritual food. In the summer evenings he would preach in the open-air, carrying his meeting into the lowest parts of the village, where he could always get a congregation of persons who never went to places of worship, and here he would preach most earnestly of Jesus and His love, always telling the 'old, old story,' until some, quite melted, would walk away to hide their tears.

"Even after this, he would frequently come to conduct the usual cottage meeting. Of weariness of body he took no notice, and when remonstrated with, he would say, 'it was the Master's work, and it *must* be done.'

"From the first, his earnestness did not cool, but grew and increased, as his spiritual life expanded. Not long before my departure, several times as he was telling his experience in the class-meeting, I could not but think of Moses's face shining as he descended from the mount, only that the shining in this case seemed rather that of the spirit from within.

"I wondered, even then, for what great end this ripening was; but, by-and-bye, when he offered himself for Africa, I thought I understood it. He spoke of it to me before mentioning it to the other members. I said, 'I am glad—sorry for the loss Denholme would sustain, for his friends too, but— *very* glad for Africa's sake.'

"At the meeting, when he mentioned it, he met, of course, with great opposition, and I could not help speaking out and pleading for Africa, begging that they would not throw cold water (speaking figuratively) upon such a grand, noble resolution of sacrifice.

"The matter was undecided when I left, but Mr. Blackburn wrote a note to say he was *not* to go. I replied to him, saying that I was sorry, as he had already made the sacrifice before offering, it would be a disappointment then *not* to go.

"I knew nothing more until Miss N——, in one of her letters, mentioned that Mr. Blackburn had sailed for Africa."

We close this section with a communication from the pen of Miss Crabtree, whose contribution has already furnished us with several paragraphs.

"He was very happy in his new sphere of labour, and delighted to talk at all times of the best methods for extending the cause of God. He was always strong and healthy in his conversation, and invariably cheerful and joyous, only occasionally speaking of his difficulties. He very seldom mentioned his sacrifices for his work as such, and then very lightly, and to disclaim any credit which might attach to him on that ground. He felt that if a man be truly called of God, the honour and privilege of such a call far more than outweigh all earthly wealth and comfort without it; and as his happiness was so great in ministering to others, he felt that he had gained much that was more valuable than anything he had lost. He never sought for merit which did not belong to him; but, as one who had made choice of a good name, he upheld his claim to what was a modest estimate of his attainments in character and knowledge, and in that particular, as in many others, he quoted Paul as his example.

"He was always reverent in his deep love for beauty of nature, and would often come from its presence in a spirit of deep humility, as if from beholding the face of God.

"My experience of his friendship was that he ever sought the highest good of those he loved, in preference to any passing pleasure for himself; yet, I never knew him allow any friendship, however dear, to come between him and his duty to God, and his work; but he was intensely sympathetic, and would witness with great distress of mind any suffering which he was unable to alleviate. In a day of heavy sorrow which came to me, he brought before me all the help he could from God's word and from prayer, urging me to a complete trust in my heavenly Father's wisdom and tenderness. His letters at that time particularly, were a source of real help and comfort, but much more so are they now, as I read them in the light of a new experience, and learn from them to look continually to the Strong for strength.

"He taught me much, and our friendship became stronger as we increased in the knowledge of God's love. We talked with each other of its power in our lives; and we walked along as pilgrims to a glorious inheritance, and often we felt our hearts to glow together as we spoke of God's goodness. Meanwhile the days drew near which brought the requirement that fresh and untried paths should be trodden by him who hesitated not one moment, but fearlessly stood forward to do the bidding of his Divine Commander."

Section II.—Fernando Po.

"THE island of Fernando Po is situated in the Gulf of Guinea, between three and four degrees north of the equator. Its greatest length is about 50 English miles, and in breadth it varies from 12 to 24 miles. It is of volcanic origin, and beautifully mountainous; indeed, when viewed from a distance, it appears as a finely shaped mountain rising out of its ocean bed, and gradually towering to a peak, the summit of which is 10,700 feet above the level of the sea. On closer inspection, however, it is found to consist of different ranges and smaller peaks, all of which contribute much to the beauty and grandeur of the whole. From the base to within a little of its greatest height the island is covered with forest, and down the many ravines and sloping valleys, formed by violent eruptions in past ages, almost innumerable brooks and streamlets may be seen adding both fertility and beauty. The soil generally is very rich and capable of yielding many kinds of tropical produce; at present, however, it is to a large extent uncultivated. The chief product is palm oil, made from the nut of a tree which abounds upon the mountain slopes. Recently coffee and cocoa plantations have been formed, and bid fair to be a success.

"As evidences, however, of what awaits the civilizing effects of Christianity, it may be said that the following articles of commerce are to be seen growing there, though not at present contributing to the exports of the place:— Arrowroot, tobacco, cotton, castor oil plant, sugar cane, and a variety of tropical fruits. At the different altitudes of such a mountainous, well watered, and fertile island, it is easy to believe that almost all products pertaining to tropical and inter-tropical lands may be profitably cultivated. At present a two-fold blight is upon the fair island; first, the indolence and entire lack of enterprise characteristic of the native tribes; and second, the debilitating and dangerous effects of the climate upon Europeans, which latter acts as a great barrier upon any undertaking involving considerable outlay of capital or lengthened residence in the country. There is reason, however, to believe that these difficulties will be diminished under the benign influences of Christianity and the increasing triumphs of science and medical skill. The climate, although not worse than that of the neighbouring coast of West Africa, is yet very trying to white people. Malarial fever is the common enemy of all our countrymen, and carries off many victims, rendering life very insecure, and a protracted residence exceedingly dangerous. We indulge, however, the hope that Fernando Po, with its natural drainage, excellent water supply, and exposure to the sea breeze, will ultimately become the most favourable place for European residents of any upon the West Coast.

"The chief town is Santa Isabel, upon the northern extremity of the island. The population of this town consists of a mixed people. A few Europeans—English and Spanish—and a number of civilized Africans, many of whom are descendants of liberated slaves, settled here when it was a British colony. The condition of some of these settlers, socially and mentally, is very low, but yet in many respects they indicate a great advance upon the aborigines of the island. For about half a century they have had a form of civilization with but few religious influences, so that morally many of them were in a most lamentable condition. The good accomplished by the Baptist Missionaries from 1842 to 1858 has never been quite obliterated, but the evils resulting from their expulsion at that latter date, and the absence of all Protestant worship for a period of 12 years, obtained for this town an unenviable notoriety. It is not boasting, but the assertion of simple fact, to state that since the opening of our mission in 1870, a marked improvement has taken place in the moral condition of both Europeans and settlers in Santa Isabel.

"At George's Bay, where we commenced a Mission in 1872, we are labouring among the aborigines, and spreading a knowledge of Christianity in a district where unrelieved heathenism prevails. The social, mental, and moral condition in this district may be summed up in a few words. Polygamy is universal, and woman's degradation complete. The people live in small wooden huts of a most wretched description. The 'native attire' consists of a small piece of cotton cloth or animal skin about the loins. They are profoundly ignorant of everything outside their own sphere, and have no knowledge of their past history save tradition. Until our missionaries acquired their language and reduced it to order, it had no written form whatever. They have a kind of devil worship, which is associated with obscene and degrading practices, and tends to intensify the dark night of heathenism with which they are cursed. Altogether their condition forms a terrible contrast to the beauties of nature around them, and forces from our lips the words of Bishop Heber,

> 'Every prospect pleases,
> And only man is vile.'

"Missionary work on this island, and especially at George's Bay, assumes the three-fold aspect of civilizing, educating, and converting, and may therefore fairly embrace all that tends in those directions. Much that at home is left with the merchant and the school-master, must of necessity be done there by the missionary, or it would not be done at all. It is his to *initiate*, so far as his time, ability, and resources will allow, anything calculated to raise socially, mentally, and morally, those to whom he is sent, and thus start them upon the upward path. Carefully avoiding whatever tends to pauperise them, or lessen any feeling of 'self help,' he needs to kindly encourage any aspiration after both temporal and spiritual improvements.

"Such work our brethren have heartily engaged in, and have seen very encouraging results. Both at Santa Isabel and George's Bay a decided impression has been produced, and Christian influences very extensively prevail.

"The prospects of our missions at Fernando Po are brighter than ever they were. The concessions recently made by the Spanish Government add greatly to our prospects of success, and we feel confident that if the Connexion will provide the means, God will raise up men who, with His blessing, will go forth to aid in winning for Christ the inhabitants of that distant isle."*

The introduction of Primitive Methodism to Fernando Po is an interesting event in the history of Missions, and aptly illustrates the guidance of Providence in indicating to the Church new fields of toil. For many years the heart of the Connexion has gone out in earnest sympathy with, and prayer for, the sons of Ham; on several occasions the proposal to found a mission to the Africans had been discussed in Conference; but deterred, either by limited resources, or by the pressure of Home and Colonial claims, no decisive step was taken, till a simple event indicated clearly and authoritatively, the will of God in the matter. A ship, trading on the West Coast of Africa, called at

---

* The above descriptive paragraphs have been generously contributed to this work by the Rev. R. W. Burnett, one of the first Primitive Methodist Missionaries to Fernando Po.

Fernando Po; and her carpenter—a Primitive Methodist local preacher—went on shore at Santa Isabel to execute some repairs of the Agent's boat. During his stay on shore he became deeply impressed with the spiritually necessitous condition of the people; and with that promptness and zeal characteristic of the community to which he belonged, he began to preach to them the "gospel of the grace of God." So acceptable were his services as a preacher, that the people urged him to remain with them, and be their minister. This was impracticable; but a memorial was prepared, and forwarded to the Missionary Committee in England, urgently asking for the appointment of a missionary to Fernando Po. In this memorial, and its associations, the Committee heard the " voice of God " calling upon them to include Africa in the range of their evangelistic labours. The fervent prayers of the Connexion had been answered, a "great and effectual door" providentially opened, and, at the earliest convenient moment, the prayer of the memorial was answered by the departure of two missionaries to Fernando Po.

On reaching that place, the missionaries were cordially welcomed, and their labours soon resulted in considerable success. In some sense, the way had been prepared for them by the work of the Baptist missionaries, who had occupied Santa Isabel some years before; and it is no small testimony to the fidelity of those converted Africans, that they had held fast their integrity during the twelve years that Protestant missionaries had been absent from the island. Santa Isabel was necessarily the base of operations; and here a vigorous and healthy church was established. " In this town, Primitive Methodism exerts a powerful influence for good; bearing its uncompromising testimony against the laxity of morals for which the place has become so long notorious, and imparting to the rising generation the elements of a sound English education. Our church there will accomodate between two and three hundred hearers . and the preaching services are generally well attended." *

From this centre, excursions were made by the missionaries to the towns in the interior, and it was not long before a second station was opened on the other side of the island at George's Bay. This is the *first* Primitive Methodist Mission to an exclusively heathen population. Here, a mission house and church have been built, school established, and religious services instituted. Fifteen converts have been gathered into church fellowship, the first fruits of a glorious harvest, it is hoped, which shall be reaped by the agents of the Primitive Methodist Missionary Society, among the countless tribes on the coast and continent of Africa.

It is probable that many of Mr. Blackburn's friends received with some surprise the intelligence that he had volunteered for Foreign Missionary work.

That he had the deepest sympathy with the great aims of missionary enterprise, and that he had numerous qualifications for effective service in it, all the facts of his public life suggest; but, in the other facts, that he was happy and successful in home work, and that by the special request of the Circuit authorities he had been appointed for a fourth year to Bingley, countenance was given to the expectation that for some time, at least, his ministry would be exercised

---

* Trips in the Tropics. By REV. S. GRIFFITHS.

in his native land. We have seen by his letter to the Rev. W. B. Luddington, in 1874, how, even then, he looked with eager eyes and throbbing heart on the prospect of going to the heathen as a missionary of the Lord Jesus; and the event which made that prospect a reality is an additional testimony to the nobleness of his nature. By the Conference of 1878, Mr. Luddington was appointed for a second term to George's Bay Mission Station, Fernando Po. On hearing of this, Mr. Blackburn expressed a strong opinion against one minister being required for a *second* term in that perilous climate, so long as many of the ministers at home had not been *once*; and hence, in a communication sent to the writer at the Conference, he volunteered for the post. As, however, the appointment of Mr. Luddington had been made, it was judged best to to let it stand, and Mr. Blackburn's offer be held over till next vacancy; but, as a sudden attack of illness prevented Mr. Luddington taking the appointment, a few weeks after the Conference closed Mr. Blackburn's offer was accepted, and, on August 10th in that year, he left his native shores to publish in a heathen land " the unsearchable riches of Christ."

The feelings entertained towards him by those who knew him best, may be gathered from the following minutes, which were unanimously passed at a largely attended meeting of the Circuit Committee, summoned to consider the application of the Missionary Committee. for his services abroad :—

"That, in the opinion of this meeting the Rev. R. S. Blackburn is well-qualified as to health, prudence, energy, zeal, and devotion for labour on our Fernando Po Mission Stations.

"That we exceedingly regret his departure from our midst, appointed, as he was by last conference, for a fourth and the concluding year of his probation to this Circuit.

"That we place on record our appreciation of the zeal and diligence with which be has discharged his ministerial duties during his three years' residence amongst us ; and we earnestly pray that divine providence may preserve his life, and crown his labours with success in the distant land to which it is proposed he should go.

"That we have a valedictory service on some convenient day before Mr. Blackburn's departure, and that Dr. S. Antliff, as missionary secretary, be desired to attend it.

"That some expression of our regard be presented to Mr. Blackburn at the above service in the form of a gift, the nature of which shall be determined afterwards."

Bingley Circuit Committee, July 17th, 1878.

The valedictory service was a memorable one. Mr. Chas. Crabtree, circuit steward, presided over the large meeting, and testified to the goodwill and affection entertained for Mr. Blackburn by the congregations both of town and country. Resolutions, expressive of appreciation and esteem, were spoken to by officials from different parts of the circuit; and addresses bearing on missionary work were given by Dr. Antliff and others. Mr. J. W. Crabtree, in the name of the various societies, presented Mr. Blackburn with a substantial memorial of the gathering, in the form of a purse, containing twenty-one pounds ; and stated that little children had contributed to it, widows had given their mite, and others struggling with poverty had rejoiced to share in the gift. In replying, Mr. Blackburn briefly sketched the work of his ministerial life, affirming that during three years he had preached nearly one thousand sermons, delivered five hundred addresses, walked over seven thousand miles, and paid nearly fifty pastoral visits weekly.

During the meeting the following lines were recited by their author, Mr. J. D. Fox, and they aptly expressed the prevailing sentiments of the gathering.

>   FAREWELL, brave soul ! Good bye, good bye !
>   Thy Master calls for thee ;
>   With earnest zeal thou dost reply,
>   Here, Lord, am I—send me !
>
>   He bids thee leave thy native land,
>   Leave kindred, friends,—leave all !
>   Thy mission's Afric's golden strand,
>   If need be, there to fall.
>
>   Farewell ! May God protect thee there,
>   In yonder heathen land ;
>   And with His own peculiar care
>   Strengthen, when weak, thine hand.
>
>   Farewell ! We soon shall miss thy face,
>   Soon parted shall we be ;
>   But often at the throne of grace
>   Will we remember thee.
>
>   When far away from those most dear,
>   Far over land and sea,
>   These words thy lonely path shall cheer,
>   At home they pray for me.
>
>   Dear Pastor, brother, friend, good-bye,
>   We hope to meet again
>   On earth,—if not, we'll meet on high,
>   And join that glorious train.
>
>   There we shall meet no more to part,
>   For ever there to dwell ;
>   And there shall we be one in heart,
>   And never say farewell !

The attitude of his mind in relation to Foreign Missionary work just as he was embarking in it, is clearly exhibited in the subjoined contributions to this work. The first, from the pen of the Rev. R. Tanfield, then of Pontefract, refers to some public services Mr. B. attended in his native town at the time of his appointment to Fernando Po; the second is by the Rev. Jas. Travis, of Liverpool, who was present at a valedictory service held in that town on the evening before Mr. B. set sail. These contributions are singularly alike in tone, and they illustrate the impression our departed friend made on most persons who came in contact with him.

Rev. R. Tanfield writes :—

" It has not been my privilege to have a long or intimate acquaintance with our dear brother, Richard Stead Blackburn, but I knew him enough to be satisfied that he was possessed, in a large degree, of the true spirit of an Apostle and Martyr of the Lord Jesus. I shall not readily forget the address he gave us at Pontefract, at the lovefeast, July 21st, 1878. The relation of his experience, naturally and properly, led him to speak of his position and prospects as a Missionary to Fernando Po. There seemed to be something prophetic in his inspiration at the time, and he appeared fully to realize it. As near as I can remember his words were these :—

" ' I have not taken this step without serious protracted thought and earnest prayer. I have considered as well as I am able the dangers and difficulties of the work and the climate. It has cost me many a sleepless night, and many a pang, to think of the dear friends I shall leave behind me. But I am sure that I am in the right path—the path of

Providence. It may be that a Martyr is required to give a proper impulse to the missionary spirit in this country, and to raise it to its proper pitch. If it be deemed necessary that I should be that Martyr, I shrink not from the sacrifice. I am ready to labour, to suffer, and to die at the work. I feel not the least anxiety about the matter. The Lord so largely sustains me by His grace, that I have no fear, no misgivings at the prospect before me. I am happy and rejoice to engage in the service of my Lord, whatever the dangers and difficulties may be.'

" All this was uttered so calmly, and yet with such depth of pathos, combined with sweet Christian simplicity and modesty, that my heart was thrilled with admiration and joy at the abounding grace God vouchsafed to His dear servant; and I could not but conclude that so precious and noble a character and life could not be laid on the altar and offered up in such a spirit without very great and glorious results. I am sure it is impossible to calculate the blessed fruit of such a life and career with such a sad but triumphant termination."

Rev. J. Travis writes :—

"I am glad to hear that you have yielded to the solicitations of your friends, and agreed to embalm in a book the memory of the late Rev. R. S. Blackburn. I had not a long or very intimate acquaintance with him, but I knew him sufficiently to esteem him. I had the privilege of taking part in his valedictory service at Liverpool, and of seeing him start for the field of battle on which he was to die.

" The last address he gave before he quitted these shores, made, I think, a deeper impression on my mind than any missionary address I ever heard. It was not whining sentimentalism, as if anxious to excite our compassion for himself, nor an inflated rhetorical description of imaginary triumphs on the mission field, and delivered, as if for oratorical effect, nor self-confident assertions, as if he were conscious of his own superiority, or else had not counted the cost of the enterprise; but a manly, intelligent, modest expression of his views of the nature and difficulties of the work, and of the motives which induced him to consecrate himself thereto. I shall not soon forget the subdued emotion, the earnest expression, the unostentatious manner, and the transparent sincerity with which he said, 'I am as certain as I am of my own existence that God has called me to this work. I am here in response to that call. "My all is on the altar." My body, soul, and spirit are His. For His sake I cheerfully sacrifice flattering worldly prospects. I know not whether I shall have great success, or whether some will call my mission a failure. I shall do my duty, cost what it may, and leave the rest to God. I may never return to the land of my birth, and to the homes of my friends; but, though I knew that I should perish in the sea, or sleep in a Fernandian grave, I would go. And whether I live or die, my going will not be in vain. I am in the Lord's hands; let Him do what seemeth Him good.'

"In my judgment a man with a nobler heart never went into our mission work. If he had lived, I have no doubt that his tact, his common sense, his Christian deportment, and his unselfish devotion, would have secured for him a place by the side of the renowned missionaries, whose names and deeds are a priceless heritage to Christendom.

"Alas! his sun has gone down before noon. He has fallen while preparing for his campaign. But his death will probably do more to intensify the missionary feeling in our denomination than anything yet done in the Connexion; and his memory will inspire missionaries with a deeper devotion, and a diviner purpose for years after many of us, who have been permitted to labour longer than he, are only remembered in heaven."

Self-sacrifice is a feature of character indispensable in every successor of the Apostles, as moral reformers and Christian missionaries. Christ demands, as the invariable conditions of discipleship, "If any man will come after Me, let him deny himself, and take up his cross, and follow Me. For whosoever will save his life shall lose it: and whosoever will lose his life for My sake shall find it."—*Matt.* xvi. 24, 25. And that cardinal virtue, required in every disciple, is pre-eminently necessary in those who toil in the high places of Christian enterprise. When the gospel was first promulgated, it filled its professors and advocates so completely with its own spirit, that to enjoy and diffuse its blessings, they cheerfully surrendered every earthly advantage they possessed; and "as many as were possessors of lands or houses sold them, and brought the prices of the things that were sold, and laid them down at the Apostles' feet." And the great work of the church demands that the same spirit live in us to-day, and that similar sacrifices be placed on her altar now. It requires men to forfeit bright prospects of temporal success, and join the ranks of those who go to distant lands, to tell the depraved and polluted heathen of a Father's love and mercy, and of a Redeemer "mighty to save." "The youth who gives himself to Christ, should be prepared to brave the cold of the North, or the burning heats of the Line, in carrying there the pure gospel; and, with the expectation that after an hour of unpitied suffering, he may lie unburied in a foreign land. The father is to be ready to part with his son—the son whose early course has been radiant as the light of a morning without clouds, and who is qualified by native endowment to adorn the bar, the bench, or the senate chamber—to preach the gospel to savages; and to lay his hand on him and bless him as the ship is loosing from her moorings, expecting to see his face no more. The mother to press her much beloved daughter to her bosom for the last time, as she leaves her native land, to meet the perils of the deep and the desert; and to die perhaps surrounded by strangers, where *her* hand cannot soothe her dying sorrows. Youths, educated with all the skill a Christian land can furnish, and accustomed to the comforts and elegancies of life, are yet to sing on many a deck as the missionary ship glides away." *

> YES, my native land, I love thee;
>   All thy scenes, I love them well;
> Friends, connections, happy country!
>   Can I bid you all farewell?
>   Can I leave you,
>   Far in distant lands to dwell?
>
> Home! thy joys are passing lovely?
>   Joys no stranger heart can tell;
> Happy home! 'tis sure I love thee;
>   Can I, can I say, farewell?
>   Can I leave thee
>   Far in distant lands to dwell?

---

* Barnes.

Scenes of sacred peace and pleasure!
Holy days and Sabbath bell;
Richest, brightest, sweetest treasure!
Can I say a last farewell?
Can I leave you
Far in heathen lands to dwell?

Yes, I hasten from you gladly,
From the scenes I love so well;
Far away, ye billows, bear me;
Lovely native land, farewell!
Pleased I leave thee
Far in heathen lands to dwell.

Bear me on, thou restless ocean;
Let the winds my canvas swell;
Heaves my heart with warm emotion,
While I go far hence to dwell.
Glad I bid thee,
Native land! Farewell! Farewell!

From the time of embarking on board the "Loanda," at Liverpool, to the closing days of his earthly life at Fernando Po, Mr. Blackburn was accustomed to make copious entries in his diary; and from this volume we quote the following:—

NOTES OF THE VOYAGE.

Aug. 10th.—"Having passed through the excitement and pain of parting from all those most dear to me on earth, for an indefinite period, 'it may be for years, or it may be for ever,' I find myself on board the steam-ship 'Loanda,' leaving my native shores to carry the blessed news of the gospel, which has made me 'wise unto salvation,' to those who are still in their sins in Fernando Po, on the West Coast of Africa. I am very thankful that God has called me to such a glorious work; at the same time I am deeply conscious of my insufficiency for it. However, God is my strength. I go in His name, and will labour, trusting in His power to sustain, and His wisdom to guide me.

We weighed anchor at four p.m. The sea was very calm; I enjoyed it in solitude, as I was in no mood for fraternising with anyone. Jesus is very near."

Aug. 11th.—"This morning I asked the Captain to allow me to hold service on board, it being the Sabbath; but he thought we had better defer it until the following Sunday, as the men were so unsettled just after leaving port. The weather continued calm until evening, when a change took place, and we had what the second officer called 'a dirty night.' About one o'clock this afternoon Tuskar Rock was passed, and we lost sight of the British Isles.

"There are only five passengers in all, four first and one second cabin; four gentlemen and one lady.

"This 'dirty night' is making deep impressions on me, and threatening me with considerable disturbance before morning."

Aug. 12th.—"Nearly the whole of this day has been spent in my cabin. I only just mustered courage to creep out this evening. The past night was full of horrors. The roaring and hissing of the sea; the howling of the wind; the screeching of the engines; the rattling of chains; the creaking of the timbers; the rolling and tossing of the ship; coupled with my own internal commotion, made matters anything but pleasant. But my hold of the Saviour is firm, so that I know whatever comes is right."

Aug. 13th.—"My health is improved a little, and I have been able to carry a little comfort to other sick passengers. We are crossing the much dreaded Bay of Biscay, and it is determined to keep up its reputation. The waves are running high, but in great disorder; first pitching us on one side, then on the other, then facing us and twisting us in all directions, making the ship pitch and roll all ways. We are expecting a heavy night."

Aug. 14th.—"God blessed me last night with sleep, but it was rather broken by dreams of the loved ones at, and associations of, home. 'Twas but a dream. I was soon aroused to the realities of my situation by a sudden lurch of the ship. However, another night is passed—as all dark and dreary nights in life pass away—succeeded by the day. We are having finer weather and smoother sea. My sickness has almost gone. I have read and talked, and walked a good deal on deck to-day, and am anticipating pleasanter times during the remainder of the voyage."

Aug. 15th.—"After a good night's rest I have enjoyed the day very much. The sea has looked grand—a deep blue colour—such a contrast to the dirty-grey appearance of the Bay of Biscay; the small waves tipped with silver by the sun. The sunset, too, was splendid; the sky so clear, and the clouds like angel's wings tipped with gold. The moon and the stars seem to shine more brightly owing to the clearness of the atmosphere.

"To-day I commenced tract distributing among the sailors as opportunity offered."

Aug. 16th.—"I have had several interesting religious conversations with the passengers. Commenced reading 'Through the Dark Continent,' by Stanley. Saw a quantity of phosphorus in the sea."

Aug. 17th.—"Arrived at Madeira at six p.m. Posted first letters home. Met with Mr. G. S——, who was distributing tracts on board our boat, and went ashore with him. He has tracts in almost all languages, and visits all vessels that call at Funchal, distributes the tracts, and where permitted, holds service. He is not engaged by any society, but does the work at his own expense, except he receives the tracts from friends. The Portuguese Officials and Roman Catholic Priests oppose him a good deal. He is a member of the Church of England."

Aug. 18th.—"Madeira now lies before us in all its splendour, looking refreshed and beautiful by the showers of yesterday. How rich the flowers and fruit look! The garden of the world has put on its best attire this morning. The town is at the base of hills towering behind it for 5,000 or 6,000 feet. It is cleaner in its appearance from the boat than when near to it, or walking its streets. In the distance are white houses, castles, churches, and villages, scattered over the sides of the hills, mixed with vineyards, clusters of trees, bananas, sugar canes, and palm trees. The variety of colour of the rocks and hills is very pleasant to the eye. Guides here are very importunate, one followed us several miles when on shore last night. This morning little naked boys came in small boats to cater for our amusement with the object of gain. Small pieces of silver were thrown into the water, when the boys would dive after and secure them, showing them with great delight on their return to the surface. All kinds of Madeira wares were brought out for sale, including chairs, Florida water, fruits, &c., and, Sunday as it is, a large trade is done. We left at eight o'clock for the Canary Islands.

"I had got permission from the Captain to hold service on board this morning, but fell sick ; however, improving towards night, I preached on the forecastle, and the congregation was very attentive. How I enjoyed this service, free from the conventionalities of modern religious society ; the officers, passengers, and crew scattered about, seated on ropes, anchors, barrels, &c., and I in the midst preaching salvation through Christ alone to men who seldom hear the ' Word of Life.' I imagined our Saviour preaching to similar congregations on the Sea of Galilee, and ' the common people heard him gladly.'"

Aug. 19th.—"We arrived at Teneriffe about noon, and anchored near Nelson's Mole at Santa Cruz. The rocky coast of Teneriffe is very grand. The rocks are of volcanic formation, varied colours, and fantastic shapes. The 'Peak' is one of the finest sights I ever saw, reaching the height of over 12,000 feet, capped with snow; and glittering in the sunshine, it was magnificent. The crater is now silent, but there are lines of black lava extending for miles, relics of bygone eruptions. Filters (dripstones) are made from the lava, it being porous. The cactus plant grows extensively here, to which the small insect cochineal attaches itself. The sale of this insect, which yields a crimson dye, is one of the principal trades of the place.

" As we were staying for a few hours, I went on shore and visited the Cathedral, in which Nelson's flag is exhibited with considerable pride by the Spaniards; next I went to the French Church, fruit market, and walked through nearly all the streets. The town is better arranged than Funchal. The churches are largely decorated with images, crucifixes, and pictures. Almost every house has its black wooden cross attached to the wall. Camels and oxen are used as beasts of burden. A few fig and palm trees are to be seen. I returned to the boat quite tired with my exertions. It is so hot ; there is scarcely a breath of wind. Anchor weighed at ten p.m."

Aug. 20th.—"Arrived at Grand Canary at six a.m., and anchored opposite Las Palmas, a very pretty town of Moorish appearance, at the foot and on the side of a reddish brown, rocky hill. The houses, like those of Santa Cruz, are chiefly built of white composition, almost like Paris plaster. The most prominent building is the Cathedral, with several towers. The island presents a very pretty appearance, with its numerous peaks of variegated rock and towns in the distance, viewed through our telescopes, looking so clean in their white garb, but like Santa Cruz, I judge, are better seen at a distance, for beneath their white exterior there lies much dirt. Canaries, poodles, and fruit were offered for sale, but not a very extensive trade was done with our ship. We took on board here a quantity of rum to curse the inhabitants of the West Coast of Africa with. We left about nine a.m. I read most of the day after leaving Canary. We are now fairly on our way to the 'Dark Continent.'"

Aug. 21st.—"Rather unwell to-day, but improved sufficiently to have service on the forecastle again in the evening. I was much amused with the Captain and Purser, who thought it must be a special fast day in the Church, as I had eaten no meat, and was holding service in the evening, it not being Sunday. This is my second service. Reading most of the day."

Aug. 22nd.—"How pretty the flying fish look to-day, with their silver coats glistening in the sunshine! How fine the sea is with its deep blue colour and silver capped waves! Everything is praising God in joyfulness and purity; only man is vile and ungrateful."

Aug. 24th.—"Passed Cape Verde this morning. This is our first view of the African coast."

Aug. 25th.—"Morning service was arranged for on the quarter-deck, but just at ten o'clock a violent storm of wind and rain—quite a tornado in force—struck us and stopped us. However, we were able to have it at 2.30 p.m., but very few attended, as it was time for sleep after lunch. In the evening I preached on the forecastle, had a large congregation, and a good time."

Aug. 26th.—"The African coast is again in sight; we are approaching it very fast. We have passed the Pilot's den, and cast anchor at Freetown, Sierra Leone. It has been said that Sierra Leone is only separated from the regions of the lost by a sheet of brown paper. Certainly such is not the impression at first sight. Hills rising gracefully to 1,500 feet above the level of the sea, covered with tropical vegetation, present themselves to the view. At eight o'clock p.m. I landed, and called upon Rev. W. Micklethwaite of the United Methodist Free Church, and was made heartily welcome to the best he had during my stay, which extended to four o'clock next day."

Aug. 27th.—"This morning I took a walk to see the 'lions' of Sierra Leone. Ascended Barrack Hill, where the military buildings are erected, and had an extensive view of the town and its surroundings. The chapels, churches, and the cemetery where so many Englishmen are laid, were pointed out to me. Returning, we called on the Rev. J. J——, Wesleyan Missionary, who accompanied us during the remainder of our wanderings. We visited the Cathedral, fruit market, Wesleyan High School, and the United Methodist Free Church School. The Cathedral is a very plain building of stone, and slated, not at all pretty, but very cool; it is said to be the coolest place in the whole colony. It is sad to see the names of so many of our countrymen on tablets upon the walls, indicating that they have died a prey to this deadly climate. At the Wesleyan High School a first-class English education is being given to the coloured youths, who are quick to learn, judging from the proficiency exhibited by two classes, one in Latin, and the other in Algebra. The master, Mr. M——, who has been educated in England, is a very nice gentleman. With true African politeness he shewed us the School, and called the boys to sing for us; they sang, "Now, pray we for our country"—very well. He then congratulated me on my appointment to Fernando Po, and on behalf of himself and the boys wished me a pleasant passage. I had the pleasure of addressing the scholars. At the United Methodist Free Church school they sang 'Jesus loves me'; it sounded so nice in their broken English. The two ministers accompanied me on board.

"We have just added a second crew to our ship, consisting of Krooboys. They are, of all the West African races, the most to be depended on for work. Several coloured passengers also joined us here. They are from Monrovia, and are returning from a tour in America."

Aug. 28th.—"Have had a long talk with the Monrovians. Have

been unwell all day. At night preached to the crew and Kroomen from ST. JOHN i. 42—'He brought him to Jesus.' This is my first sermon to Africans. Some of the Kroomen are accustomed to attend the Wesleyan Chapel at Sierra Leone, and sing Sankey's hymns very heartily. 'Hold the fort,' 'By an bye,' and 'Come to de Saviour,' went very well."

Aug. 29th.—"This morning we called at Monrovia, and received two fresh passengers :—Mr. R——, the Dutch Consul, and Mr. T——, Ex-Secretary of the Treasury for Liberia. Being interested in the history of Liberia, I soon made it in my way to have a long conversation with Mr. T——. Liberia was colonized by emancipated slaves from America in 1821, and was connected with America till 1847, when independence was declared. It is entirely governed by coloured men, but is almost in a state of bankruptcy. It is very difficult for semi-civilized people to form their own goverment, and it is quite impossible for them to manage their money affairs satisfactorily. This shows the necessity of having Ministers to superintend the districts, in Foreign Missionary work, though native agents may be largely employed. This evening we arrived at Grand Bassa in Liberia."

Sept. 1st.—"This has been a sadly desecrated Sabbath ; from early morn until ten o'clock at night we have been discharging mails and cargo to a number of ships on the Ivory Coast. The trade on this part of the coast has to be done through a few old British houses, who have ships stationed here, owing to the uncivilized state of the people."

Sept. 2nd.—"To-day we called at Grand Bassam and Assinee, on the Gold Coast. The natives are very different in features and manners from any we have seen before. The paddles they use are a different shape, and the noises they make vary. I preached this evening in the forecastle. My congregation has considerably increased by the addition of a number of deck passengers."

Sept. 4th.—"Sent letters home. We passed the Manguandah mountains. The Captain told us a story about one of them called 'Devil's Mount.' No one who ascends this mountain can live. An Englishman once set their superstitions aside and went up, but died two days afterwards. So say the natives. I preached to-night from Matt. xxii. 42, 'What think ye of Christ.' After service I and a number of passengers, Wesleyans, were singing hymns until nearly ten o'clock."

Sept. 5th.—" Hearing there was a Wesleyan Missionary at Accra, and being so tired of steamer life, I determined to land, though I had been warned of the dangerous beach. We got safely through the surf in the Government boat, with the exception of a little wetting. I made my way to the Mission House, but passing the Court House I thought I would look in there first, and heard a portion of a land case that was being tried. Upon reaching the residence of the Rev. R. R—— he invited me to stay all night, which invitation I accepted. He took me for a walk to see the sights of the town. We went about a mile along a beautiful road, commanding a view of the sea on one side, and the hills of that district about fourteen miles distant on the other. Returning we passed through many of the streets; the better ones contained a few good houses, but the majority were miserable looking mud huts, surrounded by all kinds of dirt; lean pigs and sheep running about in all directions, and articles of fetish (an object selected temporarily for worship, as a tree, stone, &c.) in abundance. My attention was specially called to one, a number of canes tied round a tree trunk, which was supposed to be a protection from lightning; but it failed, for lately the very house protected was struck, and the fetish itself destroyed. Yet such is the blind superstition of the people they rebuild their fetish along with their house. 'Country Custom,' was being celebrated; a number of people put their bodies into all kinds of unnatural shapes, and call it dancing; this was accompanied by the beating of drums and tomtoms, and yelling and singing until they had worked themselves into a perfect frenzy of excitement. Several days of this kind of procedure are devoted to their gods.

" At five o'clock I attended a female class, led by a native minister. The speaking was in the native tongue, and therefore quite unintelligible to me. I delivered an address to them in English, which was interpreted to them by the minister. At seven o'clock I led a class in English; it was composed entirely of young men, very intelligent, and some of them very pious, according to Mr. R——'s statement. The meeting was a blessed one to me, much spiritual power rested upon us.

" Accra men are much prized as coopers. They have been educated by the Basle Mission, and are very useful to the palm oil dealers."

Sept. 6th.—" Went to five o'clock prayer meeting. The people are very fervent. They sing in English, and pray in the native tongue."

"After an early breakfast I returned to the ship. We got safely through the surf. I met Mr. R—— of the Basle Mission, and had a nice conversation on mission work in general. Reached Addah this afternoon, but the surf was so bad we could not discharge our cargo Two vessels were wrecked here about a week ago."

Sept. 7th.—"The surf was worse this morning, so we went to the next place, Jellah Coffee. The ship is re-provisioned here, so we have quite an excitement—poultry dealers urging their stock as superior to their neighbours'—such a confusion of tongues and crowing of birds However, we got our supply at what in an English market would be considered a cheap rate, fowls at four and six per dozen."

Sept. 8th.—"Discharging cargo nearly all day at Little Popo. At six moved on to Grand Popo, about two hours' sail. I managed to get a service squeezed in during this short run. Oh, how Sabbaths are ignored on these boats, and how difficult it is to do any religious work. Two of the white crew seem to be profiting by the services."

Sept. 10th.—"Mr. C. V. K——, my best passenger friend, has left us to-day. He had so entwined himself around my heart, I felt his going very much. We are at Lagos. The ship is rolling so much that occasionally I find myself rolling on deck. Sharks are very abundant We can see large numbers of them swimming about the ship, but cannot catch them; they are so 'cute, one has actually fetched the bait off the hook most cleverly. I have been teaching several Accra boys to read, and conversed with them and others on religion. One of them told me that he was once suffering from small-pox when going up the coast and that they landed him at Cape Palmas. The authorities there sent him into the bush to die or get better as the case might be. He said 'Me no fit for town, dey send me live for bush; dead men bone lay for ground; me no fader, no moder, no friend, but Jesus made me happy so happy. Me sing, O, for a tousand tongues to sing, &c.'"

Sept. 12th.—"Arrived at Bonny at nine a.m. Bonny certainly belies its name, for there is nothing 'bonny' about it. It is a collection of huts thrown together in a most dismal swamp, overgrown by rank vegetation, and dirty in the extreme. If a few hours residence here does not give you the fever, you may consider yourself acclimatized.

"I went ashore and visited the Church of England Mission House, and was shown round the Mission premises by Archdeacon Crowther, the amiable and energetic son of the Ven. Bishop Crowther, D.D.

"I had the pleasure of addressing the scholars of their boarding school. This school takes charge of the children of the town, and draws them away from the follies of Ju-Juism. Mr. Crowther gave me several interesting accounts of martyrdom that had taken place there, showing the genuineness of the work.

"Domestic slavery is very common, and some of the men of Bonny possess large numbers of slaves. Some of these slaves have been converted, and of course left off their habits of stealing, lying, &c. When their masters found that this was likely to interfere with their earthly gains (as it was often profitable to the masters for the slaves to tell lies and steal for them) they determined to put a stop to their attendance at the services. One slave was told that he must cease to attend, and must steal, lie, and worship Ju-Ju as before. He respectfully but promptly refused. His master then told him that he had purchased him, that he was his property. The slave replied he would work hard, do anything for his master that was right, but sin he could not, as Jesus was his Master above the other. He was whipped and threatened with death, but still stood firm; and the threat was carried out, for after being tortured, he was thrown into the river, and died praying for his master.

"From the mission house I had to be carried through the swamp upon the shoulders of a native. As we were going I saw an iguana (a species of lizard) and requested him to catch it; but oh, how horrified he looked, and said it be Ju-Ju, meaning that it was a sacred animal. Going along the village, bits of old rag nailed to trees and bottles tied to stakes may be seen, supposed to have some virtue for warding off diseases, &c. I soon reached the Ju-Ju-house, an old broken down building made of bamboo canes, &c., and ornamented with hundreds of human skulls, the bodies having been offered in sacrifice, or slain in war, and the flesh eaten. The Ju-Ju priest came to me demanding money for the inspection; I gave him some and then had Ju-Ju palaver with him, pointing him to the true Ju-Ju the Creator of the world, and His Son Jesus Christ its Saviour. I told him that instead of asking me for 'dash' he ought to try to convert me to Ju-Juism, if it were true; but reason was nothing in his line. Ju-Juism is giving way before the influence of Christianity; as the light advances it is becoming ashamed of itself, and though its worship is still celebrated it is done more secretly.

"I saw a number of old cannons about the town. I next visited the house of Oko Jumbo, one of the head chiefs. He was from home, but his son entertained me at luncheon; and after a very interesting conversation about the future of Africa, he lent me his gig (the prettiest boat in the town) and four Kroo boys to return to the ship; which I did in true royal style. At night we had a good service on board, the congregation large, and a blessed influence."

Sept. 13th.—"This morning I went on board one of the trading hulks. These hulks have seen better days, having been used in former years for more aristocratic, though not more useful work. Now they are used as the homes and shops of British traders, who could not live long in the miserable swamps of the town. The river is very unhealthy —(one sailor has died of fever this morning, and has been laid at Rough Corner, where Bro. Hand's mortal remains lie)—much more the swamp. The beautiful ships soon fall to pieces in this destructive climate, the metal corroding, and the timber falling a prey to a worm which works very imperceptibly but very effectively."

Sept. 14th.—"Wrote letters home. Had a faithful conversation with —— about his course of life. Left Bonny at three p.m. Preached farewell sermon to-night, and said 'Good-bye' to the seamen, who all expressed regret at losing me and good wishes for my future. Lord water the seed sown among them!"

Sept. 15th.—"This morning I turned out of my cabin early, feeling anxious to see Fernando Po in the distance. At first we only discover the bare outline; but as we approach, its beautiful bay, capes and promontories are more clearly defined, and running into Clarence Cove the splendid prospect of my future home is open before me. Santa Isabel strikes me as possessing many beauties. The British flag is flying on the Consulate, the Spanish on the Governor's house; both

SANTA ISABEL, FERNANDO PO.

these are on our left. Longfield House and our Church are on the right,—the latter the prettiest building in the town; between are the residences and places of business of the traders, and the Roman Catholic Church; the houses of the poorer inhabitants behind, with Clarence Peak towering up 10,000 feet, and covered with tropical forests almost to its summit, for a magnificent background. We are anchored in Clarence Cove,—a beautiful, basin-shaped harbour, supposed to have been the crater of a volcano—an excellent harbour for vessels. On our left Point William juts out into the sea for a considerable distance, and on the right several capes afford protection. The rocks are beautified by different kinds of creeping plants, growing in rich profusion, and hanging, like festoons, over and down the cliffs.

"Bidding 'Good-bye' to all the officers in the ship, the Captain sends me ashore in his boat. Bro. Holland, in company with Bro. Brown, our coloured assistant, is on the landing stage, waiting to receive me, and my Kroomen to carry my goods to the Mission House, which is done with all speed, and after a hasty breakfast we all start for service at 9.30 a.m. Bro. Holland preached, and announced me for the four o'clock service, which I took and enjoyed. The church was full, and only five white people were present, including Mr. and Mrs. Holland and myself."

Sept. 16th.—"I forgot to name yesterday my introduction to Mamma Job and Peter Bull, of whom I had heard so much. They were a little cool in their reception of me; but the whole seemed disappointed that Mr. Luddington had not come.

"This morning I called upon the Governor, but he was out. I left my card, intimating that I would call again. About noon I received his card in return, and a message to the effect that I need not call, as he was busy. We visited the cemetery where Bros. Burnett, Roe, and Griffith's children are buried, walked along Point William, saw Governor Beecroft's tomb and the light-house. In the evening a prayer meeting was held to return thanks to God for my safe arrival. The Governor was present, and about fifty others."

Rev. W. Holland, who at the time of Mr. Blackburn's arrival was fulfilling his *second* appointment there, bears the following testimony to the zeal with which he entered on his work :—

"The day after his arrival he began to talk about going on to his own station ; but we prevailed upon him—thinking it would be for his benefit and our enjoyment—to remain with us for a week or so. And we much enjoyed his company, conversation, prayers, and influence. They did us good, for the worry, and work, and anxiety consequent upon having the care of both Missions for more than five months were telling upon us, and we needed the change and relaxation his genial presence produced. For willingness to work, I think I never met with his equal. I needed to keep him back rather than urge him on. When I went out visiting, he would accompany me, and while, as a rule, I would do the talking—for he could hardly, as yet, understand their broken English—he invariably did the praying. I would say to him on the Saturday night, 'You have to preach twice to-morrow, don't trouble to come to the prayer meeting (6.30) in the morning, but rest;' but as soon as the morning came, when the meeting had been proceeded with a short while, he would come rushing in, having most likely been roused from sleep by the singing of the first hymn. Then after dinner I would say, 'There is really no need for you to come to class ; go and rest and prepare for the public service.' It was all in vain, accompany me he would, and would have taken the service had I allowed it. Perhaps I should be compelled to go out in the heat of mid-day, and would say, 'You stop indoors ; I have been on the coast longer than you, and know how much I can bear.' His reply one day was, 'The danger is not with new comers, but with you old Africans, who having escaped so long, become careless.' There was nothing half hearted about him; in preaching, praying, singing, indeed in all the exercises of God's house, it was high pressure. Like all Europeans just out, he was out of all patience with the slow movements and the lack of energy that characterise many of the Africans; it collided so terribly with his mental and physical activities, his holy and earnest conduct. He at once won the esteem of both Europeans and Africans by his free, friendly, chatty, happy disposition, making himself just their equal, indeed in my opinion he was free to a fault. His sermons which I heard were very suggestive, but hardly sufficiently plain and simple for his African audience; but he was, I believe, greatly beloved by the people both in town and at the Bay. I do not believe the Committee ever sent forth a more earnest, devoted, plodding young man."

The annexed letter conveys his early impressions of the island, and describes the nature of his work.

" George's Bay, Fernando Po,
"October 23rd, 1878.

"My Dear ——

"I am giving different incidents of my experience of Mission life to your sister and yourself, so that I want you to read each other's letters. My time is so fully occupied that I cannot write them twice this mail. I was disappointed at not being able to see you, but it was impossible. So much for introduction.

"I.—My reception. 1.—This was not so hearty as I had anticipated, but it is easily accounted for. The people were so disappointed that Mr. Luddington had not come, they appeared unable all at once to rise above their disappointment. 2.—Yet there were redeeming features. A prayer meeting was held on the Monday night to thank God for my safe arrival, and to seek His blessing on my work amongst the Bubis. 3.—The Spanish Governor attended four of my services, but he came only as a spy; and because he found nothing in them he could prohibit, he stopped all meetings after sunset. However, we were equal to the occasion, and announced our classes and services at 4.30 instead of 7 o'clock. We are suffering a great deal of persecution. All our schools have been closed. We are not allowed to ring our bells; and in a hundred things we have to suffer petty annoyances. The closing of the schools is especially wicked at my station at the Bay, for there, there is no school at all. In the town of Isabel they have Spanish Schools. 4.—Princess Pepple was present at my first Sunday afternoon service. She is the daughter-in-law of the King Pepple who was presented to our Queen some time ago; but I find he is not of much note in Bonny, of which place he is King. Oko Jumbo is a far more powerful man.

"II.—Visit to Bassupu. Bassupu is a town about four miles from Isabel. 1.—The journey to it on foot is very arduous, being through the bush—tall entangled grass about twelve feet high, and looking like immense scythe-blades. 2.—The path is very narrow indeed, with an irregular rut running along it worn by the feet of the Bubis, and made doubly distressing by the heavy rains, this being the rainy season; there are trees to climb over, deep ravines and rivers to cross, and a blazing tropical sun throwing its rays directly upon you. 3.—When we reached the town I was so exhausted, physically, that I spread my mackintosh coat upon the floor of a house that had not been occupied by human beings since February, but which was almost alive with cockroaches, ants, and other insects. However, this did not matter, I must have rest, and down I went and slept among these nice creatures. I suppose they had famous fun out of me. 4.—When I was a little rested we went to see the King—a dirty looking old man sitting in the midst of his wives, drinking palm wine, and smoking a filthy pipe. We talked to him about Jesus, but the old sinner said he never did wrong, and that he would be all right after death. We sang, I prayed, and we then retired. 5.—My beard is a source of great attraction to the natives. They think I must be a great man, having such a large beard. They come and stroke it, and if I allow them, plait it, exclaiming, 'Sese ali' (fine very). 6.—We saw a man getting palm nuts. He appeared to literally walk up the tree, jerking himself up by means of a band fastened round the tree and his own body, then switched the branches off with his cutlass, and the women, his wives, gathered the nuts in native baskets and marched off with them on their heads.

"III.—Journey to George's Bay. My first start was a false one, for we had only just got out three miles when our main rope broke. This delayed us one night; however, we got fairly off by Tuesday morning at seven o'clock, but such was the state of the sea and so adverse the wind, that after toiling for five hours we had to run ashore at Bullen Point, about six miles from Isabel. I kindled a fire on the beach, and prepared a meal of fowl, eggs, bread, and tea. Mr. Holland, who had accompanied me so far, determined to walk back, he was so sick, and thought he should be a hindrance to us. So he, Peter Bull, and one of my Kroomen—Jack Everyday—started off in the direction of the town. I accompanied him about two miles through the bush, and then returned, but allowed Jack to go forward with him. I had a bathe in the sea, a change of clothes, and another meal. 2.—Jack having returned, we weighed anchor and started afresh. The breeze was as strong as ever, but I was determined to conquer, and I made the boys pull in the face of it; but I assure you I thought our case hopeless several times. The wind was so strong and the waves running so high we could scarcely make headway at all. We were pulling half-an-hour and did not gain 20 yards, besides the danger of our small boat being swamped. For six hours we toiled desperately, and then anchored near to Bottle Nose, about half way to the Bay. 3.—I sat on watch, and let the boys sleep, but only about two hours, and then we were off again. They rowed well until six o'clock, when they began to exclaim, 'Massa, sleep catch me;' 'Massa, work hard too much.' So I allowed two to sleep while the other two and I rowed. At eight o'clock I called the sleepers, and allowed the others to rest. We reached the Mission beach at twelve noon. I superintended the unloading of the boat and the housing of my goods, and was so exhausted I fell asleep, and slept an hour. At four o'clock I began climbing the mountain, and reached the Mission House at six. Mamma Peters had a good tea ready for me, but I was too far gone to enjoy it. I had a cold bath and went to bed. I had been without sleep since the day before at five a.m., except the hour on the beach, and in that time about twenty hours tossed about in a small boat upon the Atlantic.

"IV.—My new house is beautifully situated. Let me take you on to the piazza this beautiful evening. You are upon an elevation of about 1,500 feet, with a wide expanse of the Atlantic Ocean before you. Looking along the coast-line, you see it gracefully indented by two rounded bays, with sharp promontories, forming a w. Off the middle point stands Goat Island. The whole coast is adorned with magnificent vegetation. On your right is a long stretch of woodland terminating in Clarence Peak, over 10,000 feet high, and this evening encircled by a collar of snow white cloud, which presently deepens into crimson as the sun sinks in the Western sky. From the Peak, forming an irregular half circle round the back of my house, reaching to the left and dipping into the sea, is a range of hills and peaks. Many of them are clearly defined, and being richly covered by tropical forests, are more beautiful than the Trossachs in Scotland. You will not wonder at my naming the house 'Prospect House.'

"V.—Last Saturday I paid my first visit to King Sopo, the chief King of the neighbourhood. When I entered his palace—a low hut— he offered me a stool to sit upon. We had a talk about Christianity; I then clothed him in a royal robe—an old dressing-gown given to me for him by Mr. Luddington—telling him to wear it on state occasions, which seemed to please him immensely. I sang 'Oh, happy day, &c., then prayed, and retired. He returned my visit on Monday, and brought me a fine white fowl.

"VI.—My work here is very varied. Since I came I have built a fowl-house, made a chest, repaired two chairs, varnished a lot of furniture, preached sermons, settled disputes, superintended the farm with its numerous hands, and done a large practice in medicine. Any medical advice you can give me will be very acceptable. The people are very simple and ignorant. As some of the medicines are colourless, they thought I was cheating them and giving them water; so I made some black currant tea and coloured the water. This gives great satisfaction. One woman would not be pacified until I gave her a mustard plaster, though it was not at all what she required.

"My health is first-rate. I am happy in my work. With much love,
"Yours very faithfully,
"R. S. BLACKBURN.

" P.S.—You are such a sermoniser I thought I would divide it into sections."

Mr. Blackburn seems to have readily adapted himself to the requirements of his new sphere of labour, and to have engaged in it with all his accustomed energy. For information respecting his service in Fernando Po we are indebted chiefly to his journal, and to letters sent to England. From these sources materials are collected sufficient to illustrate the character of his work, the difficulties he encountered, and the zeal and fidelity by which his toil in the mission field was marked. We quote the following entries in his diary :—

Oct. 6th.—" This first Sabbath has been a blessed one. I preached twice, Mr. Barleycorn interpreting. The few *Bubis that are converted look so nice in their clean clothes; they are very attentive. I am surrounded by scenery of great beauty, my wants are supplied, and what is far better, I have much peace of mind consequent on the assurance that I am in the way of Providence. How I do rejoice in God. He is my all, and in all.

" Our morning prayers we make into a kind of service, as we are prohibited holding school. We sing in English, hear the verse of Scripture committed to memory, read a chapter in the New Testament, taking a verse in turn all round; we then sing in Bubi and pray in English, all repeating the Lord's prayer."

Oct. 9th.—" I am amused at the timidity of the people. One woman ran away from me when she heard the ticking

---

* The orthography of this word is somewhat doubtful. It is variously spelt: as Boobee, Boobie, Bubi. The best authorities state that when the language shall take a written form, it will be spelt Bubi.

of my watch. Children run when looked at. My first letters and papers from England—a red-letter day."

Oct. 12th.—"Sheep and goats are very religious here, and often come to prayers. Sometimes I have to stop in the middle of the reading to have them turned out."

Oct. 13th.—"The attendance at the service to-day was very good. Several of King Sopo's family attended, though he sorely abuses them for coming.

"One little boy's heart was won by a dose of medicine. He was very sick this morning, and I tried to console him, but he would have nothing to do with me ; so I gave him a dose of sweet soothing medicine suitable for his case, and he liked it so much he fell in love with me at once, and we became fast friends.

"How I enjoyed my hour on the piazza this evening, thinking of God's goodness to me in blessing me with gospel light, whilst so many are in heathen darkness. My soul is full of calm happiness. Truly 'Thou wilt keep him in perfect peace whose mind is stayed on Thee, because he trusteth in Thee.'

"We had a slight sensation in Church to-day. One of the forms broke, and threw a number of the Bubis on the floor. They presented a ludicrous appearance scattered about the Church."

Oct. 14th.—"Many of the Bubi youths are thirsting for knowledge, but because of the Governor's prohibition we dare not teach them. I feel so very sorry to say 'You cannot come,' when asked to admit them, but I believe that God will open our way."

Oct. 15th.—"We added one fresh name to our class-book to-day ; there were about twenty at the meeting."

Oct. 16th.—" Have had a long talk with a coloured trader to-day. He admitted that Christianity is right, but when urged to accept it, pleaded—like too many of my own countrymen—that he would have to give up his worldliness."

Oct. 20th.—" This has been a happy Sabbath to me. I have preached twice. How peaceful our island looked this evening as the sun was setting, and beautifying it with his parting rays. The mountain was encircled by a broad collar of snow-white cloud, gradually deepening into crimson, and then fading to whiteness, and the peak all aglow with golden fire. I wish I could send this picture home for my friends to see."

Nov. 1st.—" God has permitted me to enter upon another month in health and happiness. 'Bless the Lord, O my soul.' I pray that my work in the future may be more perfect. Visited and prayed in every house in the town of Riogorijo. Provided medicines for the sick."

Nov. 2nd.—" Huri and Bioko desire to marry, and I am anxious to introduce this Christian institution here, to give the death blow to polygamy, but fear complications with King ——, father of Bioko, who is opposed to it. I am praying for guidance in the matter."

Nov. 3rd.—" Have had nineteen patients to-day. Preached twice, and administered the Sacrament of the Lord's Supper."

Nov. 5th.—" This is my twenty-eighth birthday. I commence this year with earnest longings for a more perfect and useful life, with firm resolutions to try and attain it, and with strong faith in my Saviour's power and willingness to work in me to will and to do of His good pleasure."

Nov. 6th.—" Have been repairing the iron roof of the house to-day."

Nov. 7th.—" Whilst in service this afternoon, I saw my letters coming, which made me feel quite excited."

Nov. 9th.—" Finished reading 'Vade Mecum.' I think Homeopathy is superior to Allopathy, but it is not suitable for these people. Hydropathy would be best, if we could persuade them to adopt it, but they seem to have a dread of water and cleanliness."

Nov. 10th.—" This has been a good day to my soul. How I long for the salvation of the people. This is indeed a labour of *faith*, far more so than home work; visible results are difficult to obtain. The sand flies and other insects have been trying hard to eat me up ; however, they have not quite succeeded."

Nov. 18th.—" Have had a long and perilous journey to-day in a canoe, to make arrangements for Huri's marriage. In going, a number of porpoises crossed our path, and in returning a tornado chased us, and just broke upon us as we touched the beach; but I am deeply conscious of God's presence with me in all perils by land or water."

Nov. 20th.—" Examined the candidates for baptism. They have been attending class for more than two years, and are, so far as we know, living consistent lives. I think we are doing what our Saviour would have done under similar circumstances."

Nov. 23rd.—" To-day we have had a very interesting service, viz., the baptism of the four young people named above, followed by the Lord's Supper. A rich spiritual influence filled our hearts, and made the meeting very enjoyable. I named them Thomas Mitchell, James William Crabtree, Christiana, and Jannie Elizabeth. How nice they looked as they sat clothed, and in their right mind.

Christiana has been a real heroine. She has been severely persecuted for her religion, her father having dragged her out of Church, whipped her for attending, and even cut off her food supply; but she has been all the more devoted, and since then has been the means of bringing others. The converted people supplied her with food."

Nov. 30th.—" There has been a great gathering of the natives at Bacharicha, and under the influence of *rum*, the people are wild. England, thou hast much to answer for in this matter."

Dec. 5th.—" Mr. and Mrs. Holland, and Mrs. Hopkins, the British Consul's wife, arrived this morning on a short visit. Their society will make a pleasant change, and I trust their visit may be a blessing to me and them."

Dec. 11th.—"This has been an important day in connection with this Mission, as we have celebrated the first Christian marriage. Peter Bull and Mrs. Peters (converted coloured people) acted as godfather and godmother. This is an African peculiarity, they having to settle any disputes occurring afterwards. The Church was suitably decorated with palm leaves, ferns, and flowers. The ceremony was performed by Mr. Holland and myself, and varied by a little music, the ladies presiding at the harmonium in turn. As I gazed on the bright, happy faces of the pair, I wept for joy at the thought of their deliverance from the cruel marriage laws of heathenism. The breakfast consisted of fish, yams, and other vegetables, and the afternoon was spent by the wedding party in singing hymns."

Dec. 18th.—" This morning his Excellency the Governor favoured us with a visit, and inspected the premises and grounds. Hitherto we have only had a provisional grant of land. "Now I am to apply for a permanent one for the quantity we require."

Dec. 21st.—"Measured the land prior to making claim to the Spanish authorities for permanent grant. We had a good deal of bush to cut away, and I am very tired."

Dec. 23rd.—"Started for Santa Isabel in the afternoon. We caught a small shark in the bay. In turning Cocoa Nut Point, we touched the rocks with the bottom of our boat, but on landing soon after we found it was not much damaged. We reached Isabel at ten o'clock next morning."

Dec. 30th.—"Had a good missionary meeting. The Consul was to have presided, but being taken suddenly ill, was not able to be with us. The income is considerably in advance of last year's."

The year 1878 closed, in regard to our Fernando Po Mission, amid gathering clouds and storm. The Spanish authorities, instigated by the Romish priesthood, regard with no favour, but with strong aversion, the presence, labours, and successes of Protestant missionaries on the Island; and for some time previously a variety of petty annoyances and persecutions had seriously hampered the missionaries in their work. The schools had been closed, week-day services prohibited, except at very inconvenient hours, and a number of other edicts issued, all of which were manifestly designed to fetter and frustrate the efforts of the missionaries. The papacy is true to itself in Fernando Po as in Rome, in the nineteenth century as in the sixteenth, and is ever the determined foe of human enlightenment and freedom; and when the harassing and crippling conditions under which our work in that island has been done are remembered, the successes gained are significant and encouraging. Like the early Church, our infant cause in Africa has grown in spite of persecution, and bids fair to attain at no distant date a robust manhood. We ask for Africa, as for England, no State aid in our work. We desire none of the adventitious surroundings in which some place their confidence and boast. All we want is a fair field for our work by liberty to preach Christ's gospel faithfully and earnestly, to train the young in the principles of Christianity, and to raise the ignorant and degraded heathen by the elevating forces of Christian civilization and freedom.

On Dec. 31st, 1878, on a trivial pretext in regard to a fence in front of the Church at Santa Isabel, Mr. Holland received sentence of banishment from the island on forty-eight hours' notice. That the sentence was unjust and despotic is proved by the subsequent disavowal of this action of their representative by the Spanish Government at Madrid, and by Mr. Holland's subsequent return to his former field of labour; though the immediate effect of it was to occasion much anxiety, inconvenience, and loss, both to the mission stations and to the Committee in England.

Mr. Holland's return home, left Mr. Blackburn the only missionary on the island, and entailed on him the oversight of both stations. To a man of a cool, phlegmatic temperament, or one who would care for himself first, and the mission work afterwards, this double responsibility might have been no very serious affair; but to a man of Mr. Blackburn's energy of character, to one who never spared himself when duty called or work for the Master was to be done, such an experiment in such a climate was undoubtedly hazardous.

We quote a few more extracts from Mr. Blackburn's journal relating to the remaining months of his life on earth.

Jan. 1st. 1879.—" God has graciously permitted me to enter on another year. Oh, that it may be a profitable one in the good work I am called to do. It is likely to be an eventful one. The clouds are gathering, but I do not fear, for God is my helper."

Jan. 4th.—" Mr. Holland left us by the Loanda. I am now alone, without any earthly adviser, but my Father never fails me."

Jan. 5th.—" Attended prayer meeting at six o'clock a.m. Preached morning and evening, led class in the afternoon, and administered the Sacrament after the evening service."

Jan. 6th.—" His Excellency the Governor sent for me this morning, to enquire who was taking charge of the Church and Mr. Holland's affairs. I told him that I was. He then informed me that I had no business to open the Church on Sunday without giving forty-eight hours' notice, but he would look over the violation of the law as it had been done through ignorance. I sent in the notice, and at night started for George's Bay."

Jan. 8th.—" Had the missionary meeting at the Bay. The proceeds are about £2 more than last year. Peter Bull, Huri, and I were the speakers. The members are in great distress about my having to live in town. They look despondent, and say, 'What shall we do now?'"

Jan. 9th.—" There has been a large demand for medicines, as I have been away so long. I have made arrangements for carrying on the work of this mission in my absence."

Jan. 10th.—" Started early in the morning, and reached Santa Isabel at nine p.m."

Jan. 11th.—" Busy about many things. On the neighbouring coast another missionary has died during the week."

Jan. 15th.—" The next house to ours was burnt down this afternoon."

Jan. 18th.—" My boat returned from West Bay, bringing Peter Bull, who had been to take charge of the services until the return of Mr. Barleycorn. The Governor at once sent for him, and questioned him very closely about his doings. He asked him how he could pretend to preach. The old man replied, 'I no sabby book, Massa, but de blessed Spirit of God teach me heart, and me tell me countrymen ob de lub ob Jesus who pardon me sin and make me happy.' Palaver set."

Jan. 22.—" Have been at the Government House for three hours this morning, to receive the permanent deed for West Bay. Preached at four o'clock, and afterwards visited a number of families."

Jan. 27th.—" Started for the Bay, slept at Bottle Nose, and reached the Mission House at six p.m. next day. Attended to general matters."

Jan. 31st.—" Returned to town, starting at eight a.m., and arriving at five p.m., the quickest passage by four hours that I have made."

Feb. 1st.—" There is a general change in the Government to-day, and the Captain of the gunboat takes the ex-Governor's place, but I am informed the same laws will remain in force."

Feb. 7th.—" Visited a number of families. Collected seat rents."

Feb. 14th.—" Had a long conversation with the ex-Governor. We discussed religious and political subjects, and yet managed to keep our tempers. He expressed good wishes for my future, and assured me of his respect for me.

I wished him a pleasant voyage, and bade him adieu as he started for Spain in the 'Ambriz.'"

Feb. 17th.—"Started for West Bay this evening, but had to anchor at Bullen Point on account of the strong sea breeze."

Feb. 18th.—"Started again at two a.m., and reached Bassupu at eight; went ashore and repaired the boat; in the afternoon called at Toplapla, and reached the Mission Beach at twelve p.m., after hard struggling with wind and waves."

Feb. 25th.—"To-night I interred a child by candlelight."

March 6th.—"The second Bubi marriage on this Mission (George's Bay) was performed this morning. John Petty Sogo to Christiana Erimo Biero. They seem a likely pair to make each other happy, and to be an honour to the Mission. There was a larger congregation than usual at the service this afternoon."

March 7th.—"Started for Santa Isabel at half-past six a.m., hoping to arrive in time for the 'Nubia,' but adverse winds prevented me; hence I had the annoyance of seeing her steam out of the harbour when I was six miles away. We did not reach town until eleven p.m."

March 8th.—"To-day busy with work, which always accumulates during my absence."

March 15th.—"This evening I had a novel service, and yet a good one. One of our members has been building a house. She has just taken up her residence there, and desiring to have God's blessing on the enterprise, she wished me to go and 'say prayers.' We sung several of Sankey's hymns, I read two Psalms, and gave an address, and we prayed."

Faithful Toil. 137

March 18th.—" During the past night the most terrific tornado I have ever experienced passed over us."

April 11th.—" As it is Good Friday we had service this morning at half-past nine. Visiting the members during the afternoon."

To the above quotations we add a few selections from letters to the Missionary Secretary, and to friends in England, which may further illustrate mission life in Fernando Po.

"*Oct. 28th*, 1878.

"DEAR BRO. C———

"I am happy to say that after a very tedious journey, I reached my new station about three weeks ago. Everything appears to be in moderately good condition and order, except furniture and drapery, which soon get destroyed in this climate. Our work here is seriously crippled by the action of the Spanish authorities, and the persecuting spirit of some of the petty kings; but so far as I can judge, the small society is in a healthy condition. I have already visited several of the towns in company with Mr. Barleycorn (the Assistant Missionary), and purpose doing so regularly and systematically, as soon as I get more settled. Our morning prayers at nine are well attended.

"I would respectfully suggest to the Committee the desirability of asking young men to offer for this mission *prospectively*, and give them a few years' training. Could I have known, some time ago, that I was coming here, and have been informed of the nature of the work, I should have had the best medical training attainable, and as much intercourse with the returned missionaries as possible, to have acquired the language. This is indeed a *special* mission, requiring special qualifications and training. You have excellent men at home now, who have been in the field, and know its requirements. Bro. Parr, who has been signally successful with the language; Bro. Burnett, who has left his mark on the material interests of the mission; and Bro. Luddington, who has so won the hearts of the people. I am sure if my successor could have intercourse with these good brethren, and could study the language, medicine, and the use of joiner's tools, &c., it would be of great service to him.

"Yours sincerely,
"R. S. BLACKBURN."

"*George's Bay,*
Nov. 25th, 1878.

"DEAR DOCTOR,

"Having heard a good deal about the Mwala of the Bubis. I determined to see one; so went to Bagoricho, where preparations had been proceeding for several days. As I entered the square, one of King Loba's wives offered me a seat in the centre, and all the principal men saluted me. Those taking part in the entertainment had their skins dyed with juices of plants, ashes, palm oil, &c., in variegated colours; some blood red, others in red and grey stripes, with white spots all over their faces. Their bodies were ornamented with Bubi money, plaited grass, snake bones, and a variety of charms, consisting of bits of bone, old teeth, shells, mutton fat, &c. On their heads were large hats made of grass, with bunches of scarlet, blue, and black feathers attached. Their spears were adorned with smaller bunches of feathers similar to those in their hats, but the spears of the kings and princes were covered with long black monkey hair from the head to about the middle, in the form of a circular hair brush. Their shields are made of cow-hide, and measure about six feet by four feet. They get the skins from traders, as there are no cows here. The display commenced with a kind of march past, which was very irregular, and would have amused or disgusted military men. This was followed by various dances and cries. The shields were then seized by the most powerful men as though some unexpected enemy had made his appearance, and a sham fight with this imaginary foe began amid war songs and cries of defiance. Many war-like antics were performed, when the whole scene concluded with the return of the conquering army, accompanied with general rejoicing, the native bells, consisting of hollow wooden cases and about ten wooden tongues in each, being rung, songs of joy being sung, and by a variety of lively dances. The whole scene was wild and un-English, but not so foolish nor so wicked as the English race-course, with its betting-ring, drunkenness, swearing, and cruelty. If all the misdirected zeal of the world were thrown into proper channels, what an improvement would be made in its morality.

"On the 13th of November, Mr. Barleycorn and I, with Samuel Antliff Huri, and a Krooboy, started at nine o'clock to climb Devil's Mount, at the back of the Mission Town.

"After two hours' climbing we reached the summit. Having viewed the lake and beautiful scenery around, we sat upon some long mossy grass to dine, whence we had an extensive view of the island. Whilst thus engaged, the 'Devil man' made his appearance, looking very fierce and agitated, with gun and cutlass in hand, his skin dyed yellow and red, and charms hung round his neck. He expressed surprise that we had ventured to enter the territory of the devil without acquainting him, and bringing a sacrifice to appease his Satanic majesty's wrath. He prophesied that all manner of evil, including death, would befall us for our wickedness, and he looked very much disposed to fulfil his own prophecy by shooting us. However, he took his departure, making the woods ring with his yells and cries as he called upon Satan to destroy us. I have no doubt the devil would be glad to answer such prayers if he were not restrained by One that is mightier than he.

"When this representative of the lower regions had gone, we sang 'Praise God, from whom all blessings flow,' in English, and 'Jesus loves me, this I know,' in Bubi. Mr. Barleycorn and I engaged in prayer, and not all the evil spirits in the universe could have robbed us of the rich blessings which our Father gave us as we worshipped him there. We planted our ensign, a copy of the *Primitive Methodist*, on a tall stick, so that we might recognise the place on our return to the Mission House. We afterwards saw it through a field glass on the highest point of the mountain.

"I did not wish to return the same way as we came, so we sought another path, no easy matter in the African bush. After a time we struck a road that is kept for the devil's special use, and of course it was downwards. It led through his house, a pretty natural bower, formed by the branches of several trees overhanging a portion of the path. As we passed through it, I breathed an earnest prayer for the salvation of the deluded people of this island. At the end of the road was a large native bowl, containing two dead rats, and a quantity of rain water. We judged this was Satan's provision bowl, and that the rats had been placed there for him to eat; but he does not care for food of this kind, he prefers human souls. The rats had evidently been there a long time, they were in such an advanced state of decomposition.

"We passed through three towns, Baracharacha Bagoricho, Baracharacha Raja, and Raja, called at several houses, talked to the people about Christianity and its superiority over devil worship, and prayed with them.

"Truly the Gospel was needed here, and it is making impressions on the Bubis. Devil worshippers are becoming ashamed of their practices, whilst its priests are almost frantic. One brought me a dash of Bubi money, telling me that the devil had sent me to do the Bubis good. Is not this something like the Pharisees of our Lord's time, who said, 'He casteth out devils through the prince of the devils?'

"My health is very good. Though almost excluded from civilized society, I never was happier in my life. God is blessing me with much of His presence, and a deep consciousness of His favour. I sincerely and earnestly ask for the prayers of all my Christian brethren, that my labours may be a blessing to these poor benighted 'Devil worshippers,' who are so morally low. But whilst we pray, we must not forget to act. God requires practical as well as sentimental religious service."

"*George's Bay,*
"*March 6th,* 1879.

"DEAR BRO.

"What a number of things have happened—both here and with you—since your letter left England six weeks ago. Then we shall have to wait four or five weeks before we hear anything more. Getting letters is quite an event, as they come so seldom. The steamer comes into the harbour at 6 a.m.; we run to the post office for letters and papers, then if there be any cargo, we get the boats out, and go to the steamer and fetch it. I am a good deal better off than many poor people in England. I came from Isabel on Monday, and return to-morrow. I find it hard work looking after all these places and people. This sea journey every fortnight is so harassing. I lose two nights' sleep over the journey, in addition to the labour involved. I do hope the Committee will send out another missionary soon, or I shall 'go for die,' as the natives say, and of course I am not tired of life yet. Notwithstanding all my troubles, 'I am as happy as a king.' You know I don't stick at trifles, and the more I am opposed, the more determined I am to go forward. I often bless God for my experience at Denholme. It did me good in preparing me for my present work. I never give way to feelings of discouragement, but march straight on, doing the work nearest to my hand.

"I am sorry to hear of the bad state of trade in England, but not surprised. It is a marvel to me that trade has kept good so long with the 'liquor traffic' swallowing the earnings of the people as it has done for some years. If you do not, as a nation, shake off the accursed thing, it will swamp you."

"*Santa Isabel,*
"*April* 12*th*, 1879.

"My Dear ——

"These are exciting times at the Mission House. We are expecting   in about six weeks, and there is such a lot of preparation work to be got through. We want a new roof, the result of the heavy tornadoes we have had this season. I used to think the storms severe at Denholme, but they are like summer days compared with a tornado. You see black clouds, and hear a rumbling noise in the distance; presently the clouds get nearer, accompanied by vivid flashes of lightning. This is the signal for all living creatures to get under shelter, and for every door and window to be shut, and securely fastened. All at once there is a sound of a mighty rushing wind, which sweeps over you, tearing up trees, blowing down houses, and stripping the roofs off others in its course. One night, a short time ago a tornado awoke me about one o'clock. The house was trembling in every limb. I thought it was going to be blown over the cliff. I got up, and the rain came pelting into the house in every direction, even coming to bed to me. I put every vessel I could lay my hands upon to catch the water, and had just completed my work, and had the floor spread all over with baths, buckets, tureens, dishes, &c., when an extra strong gust of wind lifted the roof off, and I retired in disgust, with all the benefits of a shower bath. The next morning, what a wreck presented itself! The roof gone off the house—the floors and furniture covered with dirt and mud—the church roof (which is iron) partly lifted—the windows broken—the outhouses in a similar condition—the next door neighbour's house blown down, though much newer than ours. Indeed, the whole town seemed to have suffered.

"Talking of tornadoes, reminds me of an adventure I had a fortnight since, when returning from West Bay. I was about ten miles from town at eleven p.m., when one of these storms struck me without the usual warnings. My helmet and umbrella went flying, and the boat nearly capsized, and became almost unmanageable. The coast of the island is almost entirely rocky, and the few landing places are dangerous. However, I tried to land, as I knew we were not far from one of these places. It was pitch dark, the rain was falling in sheets, the wind was blowing a hurricane. My attempt to land was a failure, for very soon we were bumping upon the rocks, and after a little effort, out to sea again we go, and are driven, perhaps, three miles before the wind, when we recognise Bassupu. Now is the time for another attempt, and in we go in spite of wind and weather, though the surf did its best to upset us. We landed, and slept in a hut on the beach (being quite overpowered with our exertions, for we had been on the water twelve hours), until the storm subsided. Of course, we had no change of clothing, as everything was wet. We reached town (Santa Isabel) on Saturday morning, about half-past seven. I don't remember ever being nearer death than at that time.

"Just a word about my religious work. I have been in charge of both missions for about four months, nearly six months by the time you will receive this. Every Sunday I preach twice; conduct prayer meeting at six a.m.; lead class at two p.m.; and prayer meeting or sacrament after the evening service. Every alternate Monday night after class, which I lead, I start for George's Bay; preach there on the following day, and attend to all the affairs of that mission, and leave again on Friday morning at six o'clock, having preached twice, led class, and attended to a large medical practice ; and reach town again on Friday night or Saturday morning.

"The work for the week I am in town is this :—Monday, lead class; Tuesday, visiting for three hours ; Wednesday, preaching ; Thursday, class ; Friday, visiting (I visit the whole town periodically) ; Saturday, attend to general business matters.

"Excuse this long, wandering, light letter.

"*Santa Isabel*,
"*April* 12*th*, 1879.

"MY DEARLY BELOVED BROTHER,

"Many thanks for your letter of February. Having a few minutes, I hasten to reply, though my letter will have to be short, as I am up to the ears in business. Springing up from second man to superintendent of two circuits, thirty miles apart, is no small joke on the West Coast of Africa. Going from one to the other, every alternate week, with the thermometer at 130 degrees in the sun, is lively work, though I am not quite melted away yet ; in fact, I don't think I am an ounce lighter than when I left England. I have had no disease of any kind ; have only been bothered with prickly heat, toothache, chigoes, and a few other minor ailments scarcely worth mentioning.

"Your hope about our persecution ceasing has not been realised. Since Mr. Holland's return home, I have been the subject of many petty annoyances, but have not been fined or imprisoned.

"At present, I am enjoying peace and friendship with all the Spaniards, but their hostility to our work, though not expressed, is as strong as ever.

"With much love to you all."

We close this chapter with a communication from Rev. W. Holland, contributed since his return to Fernando Po.

"In my opinion, Mr. Blackburn was a man of *deep piety*. His self-denial, his power in prayer, his general influence, and the kind of conversation he seemed to delight in, would all lead to this conclusion. His piety, too, was of the active kind. He was not ashamed of his religion, while, at the same time, he would not obtrude it upon anyone. Of this we had evidence in coming out here. At Cape Coast Castle, we met with a young officer, who had been a fellow passenger with Mr. B. from England. He was very sorry to hear of his death, and said, ' We liked him very much ; he did not talk too much religion to us ; ' though, perhaps, no missionary has come out here who held more services on board than he. Disallowed by the Captain to hold them in the saloon, he went to the forecastle among the sailors, and conducted a service on Sundays and Wednesdays. His was, indeed, a ' Christianity in earnest ! ' For willingness to work, I think he surpassed all the men I have known ; the driving of his mind was 'like the driving of Jehu,' lashing the body on beyond its powers.

" A friend, writing to us regarding his appointment to the Bay, said, 'He is pious and plodding.' This exactly described him ; he was a real plodder. He was, moreover, thoroughly conscientious. His convictions of duty were strong. Only let him be convinced that he ought to perform a certain duty, and, if possible, he would do it regardless of consequences. Flames might rise, and floods might rage, but he would go through them to duty. Indeed, he seemed to subordinate everything—friends, wealth, comforts, health, and even life itself to the call of duty, and to be, if I may so say, a slave to his conscience."

CHAPTER IV.

Early Rest.

"For David, after he had served his own generation by the will of God, fell on sleep."— *Paul.*

"We live in deeds, not years ; in thoughts, not breaths ;
In feelings, not in figures on a dial ;
We should count time by heart throbs ; he most lives
Who thinks most, feels the noblest, acts the best."

HE last communications that Mr. Blackburn sent to friends in England, or even the final entry in his journal, gave no indications that his work on earth was so nearly accomplished. He was then in robust health, and was toiling most energetically to meet the requirements of the two stations under his care. He was also buoyant with the hope that she who had consented to share his lot in life, and who was anxiously looking forward to the time when she should join him in his African home, and be his helpmeet in the great work, would in a few weeks be by his side. He seems, till then, to have enjoyed an exceptional immunity from those attacks of disease which usually prostrate Europeans before they have been long on the West Coast of Africa. He had been able, without interruption from illness, to discharge with all his accustomed zeal the important duties of his position in Fernando Po, to take the long and perilous journey to and from the George's

Bay Station, and thus to exercise a personal superintendence of all the interests of the Protestant Missions on the island. With strength unabated, with ardour undiminished, with promising projects of further developments of missionary labour taking shape in his mind, there seemed to open before him years of fruitful and devoted service on behalf of those to whom he was sent. No premonitions of "early rest" had then been received. The future was bright with prospects of loving and consecrated toil. The sun of his manhood was but approaching its meridian, and none could have anticipated sunset before noon.

That the superintendence of the two stations on the island, all the duties of which he seems to have performed with the most rigid faithfulness, involved in such a climate a hazardous strain on a European constitution, is undeniable; but that every possible precaution against the attacks of disease was taken, or that when the disease did come, if competent medical skill could have been obtained the result might have been different, it is difficult to affirm authoritatively. What is known is this:—that by the banishment of his colleague in the work, he was left alone in the early days of 1879; that he at once undertook the double duty of superintending the two stations, thirty-five miles apart, and necessitating, as he judged, a laborious sea journey in an open boat every alternate week; that he had often an oppressive sense of solitariness and of the strain his duties imposed upon him; that he urged on the home authorities the speedy appointment of a successor to Mr. Holland, and was very desirous to resume his work at the Bay, which was seriously interrupted by his enforced residence at Santa Isabel; that when bravely struggling with the difficulties of his position, and nobly devoting himself to the interests of those he went out to serve, he was assailed by what was regarded as a temporary indisposition, but which rapidly developed into a severe malady; and that after a few days' illness, he suddenly and unexpectedly breathed his last, far away from medical attendance or skill, in the presence of a few faithful members of the infant church, and trustfully resigned his spirit to God who gave it.

The circumstances of his death may be gathered from the annexed letter, sent by the Assistant-Missionary at George's Bay, and which conveyed the mournful intelligence to the Committee in England.

"*Santa Isabel,*
"*Fernando Po,*
"*April* 24*th,* 1879.
" Rev. S. Antliff, D.D.,
"Sir,

"Am very sorry that my first letter should convey very sad news, but this, under the present circumstances, is unavoidable. You will be very sorry, and so will the other brethren, to hear of the death of the Rev. R. S. Blackburn, who departed this life on Tuesday, the 22nd of this month, at a quarter to six in the evening. He was taken ill on Monday, the 14th inst., at Santa Isabel, on which day he started in the evening for George's Bay. He considered the illness to be somewhat trivial, but on arriving at the Bay, and after a walk to the Besé, he began to feel the pain increasing.

"On Wednesday, the pain getting worse, he abandoned the idea of going to town the same week, though he had meant doing so. His suffering was great, but he bore it quietly. His illness was a severe brain fever. Sometimes he became a little delirious. On Saturday morning he arose from his bed, went to the piazza, and to the garden, but towards the evening he was down again. On Sunday he kept his bed the whole of the day. After service, we went to see him, and found him in very great pain. By his request, I read to him the first sixteen verses of the 3rd chapter of St. John's Gospel. During the reading, he was happy, and when reading the sixteenth verse, he said loudly, 'that is nice.' After we had prayed, he said, 'Preacher go die.' He also said to us, 'I am happy; I am not afraid to die.' On Monday he was able to get up, and walk to the piazza, where he spent above two hours, amusing us by telling us what had happened at Santa Isabel. Towards the afternoon he had another severe attack of the same brain fever, his head becoming so hot that the heat could be felt by putting one's hand at a distance of about an inch from him. He was so the whole night, but in the morning, though weak and rather calm, he was able to walk out. About mid-day, he took a rather long rest, until about three o'clock in the afternoon, when Mrs. Peters was roused up by his calling aloud, 'Mamma!' She ran to him, and found that he had made an attempt to rise, but was unable to do so, and, also, he was in an unconscious state of mind, his eyes partly closed. Mrs. Peters tried her very best to arouse him, by administering hartshorn, but all was in vain. About a quarter to six in the evening, he breathed his last. When he died, the boat not being there, Mr. Vivour, at our request, lent us a boat, in which we took the body to Santa Isabel, where we arrived on Wednesday, about half-past six. The same night carpenters made the coffin, and he was buried in the morning at about eight o'clock. Mr. Brown, the Assistant Missionary, read the Burial Service. To-day has been a day of great weeping at Santa Isabel, as yesterday and the day before had been at George's Bay, for the Bubi Christians and ourselves wept for the loss we had sustained; and here, at Isabel, the weeping is great. After burial, the Spanish authorities sealed the house door first, and next the Church door, and, I learn, the same fate awaits our George's Bay Mission. 'Oh, Lord! help us.' Their plausible reason for doing so, as Mr. Brown told me just now, is, their not knowing of anybody that is empowered by the Committee to see after the property; that we are only employed by the men out here, and not directly by the Home Mission. I am going to the Bay to-morrow, and will still go on until I am stopped. I am sorry on account of the work, especially George's Bay Mission. I shall still be doing what I can, even though they close all the Churches, and the Mission House.

"May I just say here, that I think Mr. Blackburn's brain fever was occasioned by his frequent exposures to the weather, when he was not sufficiently acclimatized. During the time Mr. Holland was here, Mr. B. was quite well, but since Mr. H. left, Mr. B. has had to come to the Bay every two weeks and-a-half, and stay over two days, and then back again; and, all praise to him, he has never missed a single trip to the town. He was very laborious in visiting from house to house, not excepting the houses of those whose creeds were directly opposed to his; and this very often under the heat of a blazing sun. A deputation of old matrons waited on him one day, begging him to be more careful of himself, for his health's sake ; and, secondly, for the good of the Church. Among these old women, was old Mamma Job, well known in this place for her piety and good sense.

"May God comfort the relatives of our dear departed minister, and also bless this visitation of His providence to their good, and may the Committee and Churches be comforted and strengthened by Him. Our cry just now is, 'Come over and help us.' Can any of the missionaries that have been out before come again? This would be very answerable under the present circumstances, for if a new man come out, there is no minister here to advise him. There are Europeans here, but the kind of advice that a missionary most needs I don't think they can give him. Hoping you will write this sad news to the bereaved father, with many words of comfort, and may yourself be comforted and strengthened,

"I remain,
"Yours in the Gospel,
"W. N. BARLEYCORN."

The same writer, in a letter to Mr. Blackburn, of Pontefract, the bereaved father of the deceased missionary, says :—

" Mr. Blackburn.

"DEAR SIR,—With great reluctance I am now writing to you, and may our heavenly Father grant you strength to receive what, in His providence, He has seen fit to impose on you. I am sorry, indeed, to inform you of the death of our worthy minister, and your dear son, the Rev. R. S. Blackburn, whose end was peace. During his nine days' illness he was always happy, and expressed himself undoubtfully that he was resting upon a loving Saviour. He was taken ill on Monday evening, at Santa Isabel, of a very light head-ache; but, looking upon it as a very trifling illness, and not wishing to omit doing his duty, he started the same evening for the Bay, which he reached on Tuesday evening, April 15th. Since then he principally kept his bed until Tuesday, the 22nd, when he died at a quarter to six in the evening. We took him to Santa Isabel, the capital, and there, followed by many weeping acquaintances, both black and white, he was decently committed to the last appointed home for all mortals. I have no doubt that, painful as this loss is to us, yet God is glorified, for the Bubis, among whom he laboured successfully, have learnt a great lesson, which is, the joyful and triumphant death of a Christian man. May you be comforted and upheld by the hand which never errs in dealing with His servants, is the wish of,

"Yours in Jesus Christ,
" WILLIAM N. BARLEYCORN,
" *Missionary Assistant at George's Bay.*"

The following selection is from a letter sent by a white trader on the island :—

"Although your dear son has been so short a time amongst us, I think it impossible for anyone to have secured such an amount of respect and affection, on all sides, as he had, in less space of time. Your dear son's body was carried to its last resting-place, covered by his country's flag, and followed by a sorrowing populace, and was interred at 8 o'clock a.m., most decently, in a well-dug and very dry grave, in a good position. The Connexion's burial service was also solemnly read over it. He was opened and examined by a Spanish doctor, to see if he had died of poison, or any other unnatural cause."

The intelligence of the sad event by which the churches in Fernando Po, Mr. Blackburn's friends, and the Connexion at large had sustained such a painful bereavement was received in England with profoundest concern. That his mission was a perilous one was well known ; but as each of his predecessors in that sphere of toil had been permitted to return, though with shattered health, and as several had served a second term there, it was earnestly hoped and believed that his strong frame would bear the strain put upon it. Such hopes were doomed to bitter disappointment; and thus another noble life has been offered on the altar of Africa's emancipation, and another name added to the long roll of those who have suffered and died in her cause.

On the outward voyage, the following lines, along with an autograph, were written in Mr. Blackburn's album, and they might form a not unsuitable inscription for his own tomb :—

"AN EPITAPH.

"Here lies a soldier whom all must applaud,
He fought many a battle at home and abroad ;
But the hottest engagement he ever was in,
Was the conquest of self in the battle of sin.

"May your last abode, after a long and useful career, be worthy this epitaph ! You have come here to do battle with the most formidable armies of sin, and will have to exercise great self-control, patience, and love. May God help you to overcome all foes, for His glory and the good of Africa !

"*Bonny River, Sept. 12th, 1878.*"

Immediately on learning the mournful fact of Mr. Blackburn's death, the Missionary Secretary wrote the subjoined letter of sympathy to the bereaved parent :—

"*London, June 3rd,* 1879.

"MY DEAR SIR,

"On my return home late last night, I was deeply pained to hear of the decease of your son at Fernando Po. It is a mysterious Providence. I fear he has attempted too much work. I have, in my two last letters, urged him to take great care of his health, and promised to send out someone to help him as soon as we could find a suitable man to fill the place. At the same time he wrote to say: 'Health good.' 'Very well,' and so on. We hoped that his health would be continued; but the Allwise Disposer of events has otherwise decreed. I deeply sympathise with you in your great affliction, and hope sustaining grace will be imparted to you.

"Your son's letters always did the General Missionary Committee a great deal of good. They had in them the true missionary spirit, and withal, were so full of hope as to the future of the mission. We have lost a valuable missionary, you have lost a noble and loving son; but heaven has received a pure and glorified spirit, 'Absent from the body—present with the Lord.'

"I am, yours truly,

"WILLIAM CUTTS."

Not long after the receipt of the sad news, a memorial sermon was preached by the writer at Bingley, Pontefract, and other places, from the text, " But none of these things move me, neither count I my life dear unto myself, so that I might finish my course with joy, and the ministry which I have received of the Lord Jesus, to testify the Gospel of the grace of God."—Acts xx. 24.

At the request of the friends the sermon was afterwards published in a pamphlet form, under the title of "Heroism in Missionary Service;" and from this production a few paragraphs are transferred to these pages.

"It is not permitted us to choose the time or the circumstances under which our course shall end. If this liberty were granted, we should probably select a green old age, and a circle of attached and appreciative relatives and friends. God often appoints otherwise. *How frequently devoted lives close early!* God seems to take soonest those whom He loves the most. The purest lives are often the shortest. The most useful men often do their work in the briefest space. Men live not merely in the length of their days, but in the pureness of their thoughts, in the nobleness of their deeds, in the heavenliness of their character and service. Some of the greatest careers the world has seen, have been short in point of time, but deep and penetrating in the influence they wielded, and world-wide in the results they produced;—meteor-like in the brevity and brilliancy of their existence. John the Baptist's ministry covered but a brief space in a human life; but how mighty in its character! how glorious in its announcements! how stupendous in its issues! Christ's personal ministry was limited to three or four brief years; but how full those years were! Sometimes a man's life-work may be done, and done nobly, while others are dreamily thinking about theirs, or leisurely preparing for it. God's 'ways are higher than our ways,' and 'His thoughts than our thoughts;' and often when the sun of a man's life seems to be at its meridian, it is suddenly eclipsed, but only to shine with greater brilliancy in another clime.

"*And sometimes most valuable lives terminate almost in solitude.* Under no circumstances can the presence of beloved friends be more prized, or the alleviations which their kindly offices afford be more welcome, than in the hours of sickness and approaching death. Then, if ever, we want loving hearts to sympathise with us, willing hands to minister to our necessities, and gentle voices to whisper words of comfort and hope in our ears. Who does not wish to be surrounded by loved ones when death comes? They may not go with us into the 'Valley,' but they may point to the 'Delectable Mountains,' and the 'Heavenly City' beyond. 'The last enemy' must be encountered alone; and the heart fortified with Christian faith, and cheered by a 'lively hope,' will not fear the encounter; the foe has been vanquished by the Great Captain of our salvation, and through that conquest all His followers will be victors too. Yet inexpressibly welcome in our closing hours must be the presence and solace of our dearest friends. But, in the providence of God, it is sometimes otherwise appointed, and, after signal service and success in the Redeemer's cause, it happens that devoted lives close in solitude. The death of Livingstone at Ilala, Central Africa, thousands of miles from friends and kindred, after a life of rare devotedness to the interests of humanity, is one of the most touching events in human history. His faithful followers, though their fidelity was proved, unmistakably, by the reverent care with which his remains were conveyed for 1500 miles to the shore, and then sent to his native land, could scarcely meet the necessities of the hour. He lived nobly, and died almost alone. And so our departed friend met the final foe almost alone; kindred, friends, country, thousands of miles away. The Assistant Missionary, and a Matron of the Church, furnished to him all the alleviations their sympathy and services could afford; still, almost alone he died—and yet not alone. In ancient times, when three moral heroes were 'cast into the burning fiery furnace,' on account of their fealty to conscience and to God, there was a 'fourth' seen in the fire with them, 'like unto the Son of God.' His presence delivered them, so that when taken out, 'not even the smell of fire had passed on them.' So, in our friend's dying hour, Christ was with him, sustaining by His power, cheering by His presence, and, when earth faded from vision, opening heaven to his wondering and enraptured gaze. He has gone from our midst, and we mourn his early removal, but we rejoice in the assurance that he has entered into rest. 'That only is truly lost which we have ceased to love. Our griefs of bereavement, our expostulations with death, too often treat as utterly gone, treasures, whose best portion is with us still, even proved to be present, by the very tears that weep their absence. Of all the ingredients that enter into that complex thing, a human life, of all the influences that radiate from it, none surely are so essential as the affections it kindles in others; and if beings around entertain of it a blessed and noble conception, are filled by it with generous aspirations, and feel the thought of it to be as a fire from heaven, *in this* is its true and best existence. And *all this* does death leave behind, as our indestructible possession; from our mere eyes he takes the visible form of the objects of our love; for *this* is *only* borrowed; from our souls he cannot take the love itself, to which that is subservient; for it is given us for ever. The very grief that wastes us, testifies that in his true worth, the companion we lament as lost, is with us still; for is it not the idea of him that weeps in us, his image that supplies the tears? His best offices he will continue to us yet; with serenest look he will rebuke our disquiet, brace our faith, quicken our conscience, and cool the fever heats of our life. The sainted dead shall finish for us the blessed work which they began. They tarried with us, and nurtured a human love; they depart from us, and kindle a divine. Cease then our complaining hearts, and wait in patience the great gathering of purified and glorified souls.*"

The subjoined lines—though referring to another sphere of missionary toil—aptly and beautifully express the needs, prospects, and perils of missionary labour in Western Africa.

> I came from a land where a beautiful light
>   Is slow creeping o'er hill-top and vale;
> Where broad is the field, and the harvest is white,
>   But the reapers are haggard and pale.
>
> All wasted and worn with their wearisome toil,
>   Still they pause not—that brave little band!—
> Though soon their low pillows must be the strange soil
>   Of that distant and grave-dotted strand.
>
> For dangers uncounted are clustering there;
>   The pestilence stalks uncontrolled;
> Strange poisons are borne on the soft, languid air,
>   And lurk in each leaf's fragrant fold.

---

* Martineau.

> There the rose never blooms on fair woman's wan cheek,
>   But there's a beautiful light in her eye ;
> And the smile that she wears is so loving and meek,
>   None can doubt it comes down from the sky.
>
> There the strong man is bow'd in his youth's golden prime,
>   But he cheerily sings at his toil ;
> For he thinks of his sheaves, and the garnering time
>   Of the glorious Lord of the soil.
>
> And ever they turn—that brave, wan little band—
>   A long, wistful gaze on the west—
> Do they come, do they come, from that dear distant land,
>   That land of the lovely and blest?
>
> Do they come? do they come? O, we're feeble and wan,
>   And we're passing like shadows away ;
> But the harvest is white, and, lo ! yonder the dawn !
>   For labourers—for labourers we pray !—*Mrs. E. C. Judson.*

There is one other event to which allusion must be made before this chapter closes. When Mr. Blackburn left England he was unmarried ; but it was arranged that at an early period the young lady to whom he was engaged should go out to him, and that they should be married at Fernando Po. The circumstances of her family were such as to make it *exceedingly* inconvenient for her to leave England at the time he set sail, or their marriage would, in all probability, have preceded his departure. It is true that Mr. Blackburn's ministerial probation was not expired by nearly twelve months ; but this would have been no barrier to their immediate union had other events been favourable. In a letter written to the Missionary Committee during the negotiations previous to Mr. Blackburn's appointment to Fernando Po, and in reply to certain enquiries, respecting it, he says :—

"My decision is not the impulse of the moment. For some years my heart has been drawn to the Fernandian Mission, but I have not dared to name it, lest I should move in advance of Providence. Hence I was waiting until your Committee should call.

"The second part of your question is rather more difficult to answer. The lady to whom I am 'engaged,' has recently lost her mother by death, and she is her father's housekeeper. Her brother is very ill, and requires her constant attention at present; so that I do not think she would be at liberty to marry immediately. She does not object to my going, nor to accompany me when my probation closes; but your question puts the matter in a light that I have not brought before her. I am writing to her by this post, and will tell her what you say; probably I shall have a reply in a day or two."

It was found, however, that circumstances required her presence in England for a few months longer, so arrangements were made that he should go alone, and that she should join him in his African home at the earliest convenient period. He sailed in the autumn of 1878; and in the ensuing spring, the way having opened for the completion of the arrangement, she made preparations to follow him. Suitable companions for the voyage having been secured, she embarked on April 26th, 1879, totally ignorant of the dreadful fact that four days previous he had breathed his last.

His letters indicate how, that as the time of her expected arrival approached, he looked forward to the event with bright and buoyant hope; and that he anticipated her presence would furnish him with the companionship his social nature craved for, and her counsel the help his trying circumstances, required. That such hope, under such circumstances was doomed to disappointment, is one of the inscrutable mysteries of life.

Regrets are unavailing, but for the sake of the Missions in Fernando Po, it is difficult to repress the wish that Miss Crabtree had been permitted to join the lonely and earnest toiler in that distant part of the Lord's vineyard. Mentally, socially, and morally, her qualifications for service in the mission field are of no ordinary character, and her influence on her own sex among the Bubis, must have been of considerable extent, and of a refining and elevating nature. It is not unlikely that the ministry of woman is as necessary for the social elevation of some of the degraded tribes of Africa, as that of man; and in the past, woman has proved herself capable of signal service for the Master. "The weaker sex gave to Israel as many heroines and holy women, as valiant servants of God; Paganism itself strove in vain to deprive woman of her dignity, for many a Greek and Roman mother showed that she had a heart as valiant as her son's. The royal roll of martyrdom shows the names of Christian women as well as men. The wife could face torture and death no less bravely than her husband, and shares equally with him the glory and the honour that belong to all who die for liberty and virtue. Heroism is no monopoly of the masculine nature; it is the appanage of every noble soul, and confers its patent of moral nobility on all who show themselves capable of it."*

---

* "The Early Years of Christianity." E. D. PRESSENSE.

Early Rest.

The annexed singularly touching and beautiful communication, from the pen of Miss Crabtree, explains itself, and can scarcely fail to minister to the consolation and trust in God of all who in times of bereavement and trial read these pages:—

"The last week before his departure to Africa I spent in his company, and we held solemn converse together before God; and I hope I shall never lose the blessed influence which came from what I witnessed then, as I stood in the presence of a heart completely consecrated to God's work; such depth of humility—such imploring for strength sufficient for the sudden and mighty need—such burning love for God and the souls of those who need salvation—and mingled in it such strong human emotion; but all crowned with a calm and unshaken trust in the power of an Almighty God. Little was said, but much was felt and thought; and on the mission altar, life and love were laid. The cost was counted, and had fires burned around, or waters have yawned before, it is no fancy of mine, but a firm conviction, that nothing would have held him back who was convinced that the Lord of heaven and earth had said to him—'Go forth!'

"In those last hours were mountain-top communings in the secret place of the Most High, and peace and power filled to overflowing the soul of him whom we loved, and whom we sent out from our presence with fervent breathings to God that he might be used for His highest purpose. We did not know, nor would we if we could, the road which lay before, but I promised to join him in his African home directly the way should open for me to do so. Among his last words, he said to me very impressively—'You must trust in God, Jannie, whatever comes, and He will never leave you; He will always care for you.' Yet we never talked of death, for we hoped for life, and calmly and trustingly we said—' Good bye!' Thus he left us, with holy words of benediction; and it was fitting it should be so. They will ever remain with me until the evening-time, when God will lead us home, and we shall sit down together at the Marriage Supper of the Lamb.

"According to the request of the biographer, I must now come to speak of myself, and how I was brought to hear the crash of my hopes for this life. I would rather not publish it in this way, and I would much rather not bring myself to the front, in connection with the noble life held up to the public; but if my doing so will be of any service in lending interest to the close of that life, I will, for that reason, gladly do my part. And I should like to tell those whose prayers went up so earnestly on my behalf, how the answer came; and I should like, most of all, to glorify my God, whose presence did not fail me when I passed through the waters.

"I started for Fernando Po on the 26th of April, 1879, in the steam-ship *Volta*, with Mrs. Fuller, the wife of the Rev. J. J. Fuller, of Cameroons, as my companion. There were eight of a missionary party, in addition to ourselves; and among them the Rev. T. J. Comber and his colleagues for the Baptist Mission on the Congo.

"The Captain and officers were kind and gentlemanly, and the remaining passengers were such as to make our ship's company an unusually agreeable one. The weather was very favourable, and we promised ourselves a pleasant voyage.

Early Rest.

"At the end of three weeks we reached Sierra Leone, where Consul Hopkins was then staying. He came to see me, bringing a letter which had been enclosed in one to himself, assuring me of a hearty welcome, and speaking brightly of the good health of the writer. Consul Hopkins promised to follow me by the next steamer, and told me of arrangements which he had thoughtfully made for my comfort. Four days later we came near to Cape Coast Castle. My text that morning, from my daily text book was, 'Take My yoke upon you;' and the verse of poetry following :—

> 'Teach me to do Thy will;
> Meekly to bear Thy yoke,
> Gladly to drink Thy bitterest cup,
> To bear Thy keenest stroke!'

And that day God dealt out to me the keenest stroke of my life. Just after luncheon, we sighted the *Gaboon*—a homeward-bound vessel. Captain Monro and one or two others went aboard her, and in a very short time we noticed a small boat coming from her, with a gentleman to visit us. He came on board, asking for Mrs. Fuller, and was announced as the Rev. A. Ross, from Calabar. I directed him to her, and in a little while, as I sat in the ladies' cabin, I heard low sobs of grief proceeding from the saloon. I hesitated a short time, and then went in and found Mrs. Fuller weeping uncontrollably, with Mr. Ross sitting by her side. I trembled, fearing some sad news had been told her of her husband, and begged her to inform me; but as she could not speak, I put my arms around her, hoping to soothe and comfort her. Suddenly, in a burst of deep anguish, she clasped me to her, and sobbed in my ears the words—'My darling, you must go home! Oh! my darling child, you have to go back again!'

Somehow I got to Mr. Ross, and, after what seemed a long time, he tenderly and gently replied to my questions, and told me what was sufficient to make me feel, that he who had so long waited in patient and loving trust for my companionship, no longer needed me.

"With a cry to God for pity and help, I tried to realise it, and what it meant. To me it was the same as if the earth had given way, or the sky had fallen. I wished for nothing. The arrow had pierced to the core of my heart, and I was completely stricken and wounded; yet a deep awe rested on my spirit. I knew that the Divine Presence was nearer to me than it had ever been before, and I said—'It is God! He has done it, and He will tell me; I will wait, and let Him speak to me.' Soon I heard voices urging me to get ready for transhipping, as we must separate speedily. I obeyed, and hurriedly put together my things, with the assistance of all around me. Then it struck me, I might still go on to Fernando Po, and see if there was anything which I could do; but the friends said 'No,' imperatively, and hastened on my preparations. I was too much stunned to think, and it did not matter to me where I went, or with whom; so I proceeded with my preparations, and very soon I felt myself lowered from one ship, and lifted into another. As I was leaving, I saw dear Mrs. Fuller, who had been so kind and tender to me, and so full of sympathy for me in my hopes, weeping and sharing with me my grief. She waved her adieu, and the others spoke their farewells. As I went among the fresh faces, a kind sisterly hand was extended to me to lead me to a quiet refuge, where I might, undisturbed, moan out my cries to my Father in heaven.

"We moved off, the hours passed along, and Mrs. Ross

came to me to read a few verses of the 14th chapter of St. John's Gospel, and then left me.

"Oh! how I would urge every one in the darkest hour of trials to go immediately to God for strength and comfort; for, most assuredly, He gave them to me. The same hand which applied the pruning knife, applied the healing balm. He showed me how, long before, I had offered my all to Him for Africa's sake, and now He had accepted it; how I had agreed to live or die, to suffer or sorrow, if only His will might be done, and now the opportunity was come. My service was not needed, but my trust was, and my willingness to resign cheerfully my hopes of earthly happiness, and to leave my future in God's hands were required at once. I saw that in yielding up, without a murmur, what was dearest, I might give to the Saviour such a costly alabaster box of precious ointment, as I never could have done in my poor services, and so I gave it to Him. I saw Him as my dying Lord, standing alone in the 'Garden of Gethsemane,' suffering for me, and again drinking the bitter cup, saying to me by His looks—'This is all for you; will you not for My sake, and for the sake of the perishing one's of Africa, share with Me the bitter draught?' With quivering heart I said, 'Yes, Lord, I will—to the last and bitterest dreg if Thou wilt give me strength, and stand beside me!' So I drank. I thought of how I might have been allowed to stand by the dying form, if only it had been in time to lay my hand on the burning brow, and speak the word of comfort in his ears; but I said, it must be best not. I thought of the sacrifice to the Church, as well as to me, but I said it must be best; God would never have allowed the sun to scorch him, but to serve some useful purpose. I thought how wise God was, and I was determined to believe in Him; yet my heart would bleed and ache, and I knew not how I must live; when one evening I saw the everlasting arms of my Father God stretched out to me, and in tones of tenderest love I heard him say to my soul—'My child, am I not sufficient for all thy need? Human care and protection are lost to thee, but is not Divine Love left in all its rich fulness? Come nearer to Me, and thou shalt always be shielded and cared for.' And listening, I was comforted. I went nearer to Him, and took to myself the promises of my blessed Bible. As I was taught, so I learnt, that it was a blessed privilege to lay down my wreath of orange-blossom at the feet of Him who, for my sake, wore a crown of thorns; and that in perfect acquiescence there is perfect rest. So from my heaviest grief came my deepest joy.

"For the one who has gone, we may not, must not mourn. He is happy beyond all thought; and now instead of waiting under the palm-trees of an African shore, I know he will welcome me beside the crystal sea in the City of God; and there when 'the day shall break and the shadows flee away' we shall meet.

"Oh to be faithful to our stewardship as he was faithful.

"I thank God each day for the legacy of sweet memories that is left to me. It never fails to help me in my lowly duties, by giving me a longing for that of which it is most fragrant, viz. :—the strong, loving purpose to be faithful unto death; and I thank God each evening that

> 'This sweetly solemn thought
>   Comes to me o'er and o'er;
> I'm nearer my home to-day,
>   Than ever I've been before.

> Nearer my Father's house,
>   Where the many mansions be;
> Nearer the great white throne,
>   Nearer the crystal sea.'

Surely God is leading home all who love Him, and do His will, and then He will wipe all our tears away, and unfold to us the mystery of His great plan. Until then, I will trust and hope for the future, and rejoice in the present, for 'the Lord Jehovah is my strength and my song.'

"On my journey outward, I had lent to me a volume of Frances Ridley Havergal's poems, and I copied from it into my scrap-book two or three pieces which struck me as being exquisitely beautiful in their expression of some of the deepest truths and experiences of this life. As I came back homeward bound, one of them was continually in my mind, and seemed to me as a sacred message from God, though only a repetition of all I had read in the promise-roll of His word, and it acted upon my spirit as I would like that it should upon many another, and therefore I venture to send it for insertion, so that those who read this may also read—

COMPENSATION.

Oh, the compensating springs! O the balance-wheels of life,
Hidden away in the workings under the seeming strife!
Slowing the fret and the friction, weighting the whirl and the force,
Evolving the truest power from each unconscious source.

How shall we gauge the whole, who can only guess a part?
How can we read the life, when we cannot spell the heart?
How shall we measure another, we who can never know
From the juttings above the surface, the depth of the vein below?

Early Rest.

Even our present way is known to ourselves alone,
Height and abyss and torrent, flower and thorn and stone ;
But we gaze on another's path as a far-off mountain scene,
Scanning the outlined hills, but never the vales between.

How shall we judge their present, we who have never seen
That which is past for ever, and that which might have been ?
Measuring by ourselves, unwise indeed are we,
Measuring what we *know* by what we can hardly *see*.

Ah ! if we knew it all, we should surely understand
That the balance of sorrow and joy is held with an even hand,
That the scale of success or loss shall never overflow,
And that compensation is twined with the lot of high and low.

The easy path in the lowland hath little of grand or new,
But a toilsome ascent leads on to a wide and glorious view ;
Peopled and warm is the valley, lonely and chill the height,
But the peak that is nearer the storm-cloud is nearer the stars of light.

Launch on the foaming stream that bears you along like a dart—
There is danger of rapid and rock, there is tension of muscle and heart ;
Glide on the easy current, monotonous, calm, and slow,
You are spared the quiver and strain in the safe and quiet flow.

O the sweetness that dwells in a harp of many strings,
While each, all vocal with love, in tuneful harmony rings !
But O the wail and the discord, when one and another is rent,
Tensionless, broken, or lost from the cherished instrument.

For rapture of love is linked with the pain or fear of loss,
And the hand that takes the crown must ache with many a cross ;
Yet he who hath never a conflict hath never a victor's palm,
And only the toilers know the sweetness of rest and calm.

Only between the storms can the Alpine traveller know
Transcendent glory of clearness, marvels of gleam and glow ;
Had he the brightness unbroken of cloudless summer days,
This had been dimmed by the dust and the veil of a brooding haze.

Early Rest.

Who would dare the choice *neither* or *both* to know,
The finest quiver of joy or the agony-thrill of woe?
Never the exquisite pain, then never the exquisite bliss,
For the heart that is dull to that can never be strung to this.

Great is the peril or toil if the glory or gain be great;
Never an earthly gift, without responsible weight;
Never a treasure without a following shade of care;
Never a power without the lurk of a subtle snare.

For the swift is not the safe, and the sweet is not the strong;
The smooth is not the short, and the keen is not the long;
The much is not the most, and the wide is not the deep;
And the flow is never a spring, when the ebb is only neap.

Then hush! oh, hush! for the Father knows what thou knowest not,
The need and the thorn and the shadow linked with the fairest lot;
Knows the wisest exemption from many an unseen snare,
Knows what will keep thee nearest, knows what thou could'st not bear.

Hush! oh, hush! for the Father portioneth as He will,
To all His beloved children, and shall they not be still?
Is not His will the wisest, is not His choice the best?
And in perfect acquiescence is not there perfect rest?

Hush! oh, hush! for the Father whose ways are true and just,
Knoweth and careth and loveth, and waits for thy perfect trust;
The cup He is slowly filling shall soon be full to the brim,
And infinite compensations for ever be found in Him.

Hush! oh, hush! for the Father hath fulness of joy in store,
Treasures of power and wisdom, and pleasures for evermore;
Blessing and honour and glory, endless, infinite bliss;—
Child of His love and His choice, oh, can'st thou not wait for this?

CHAPTER V

Fragrant Memories.

"In My Father's house are many mansions. I go to prepare a place for you."—*Jesus Christ.*

"To die is gain."—*Paul.*

"What though the mast be now blown overboard;
The cable broke, the holding anchor lost,
And half our sailors swallowed in the flood,
Yet lives our PILOT still."

SECTION I.—ESTIMATE OF CHARACTER AND MINISTRY.

"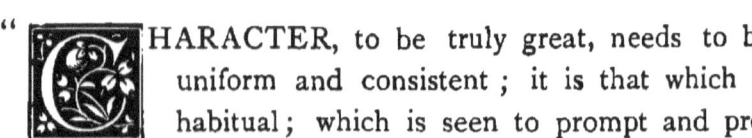HARACTER, to be truly great, needs to be uniform and consistent; it is that which is habitual; which is seen to prompt and preside in ordinary duty as well as in remarkable emergencies. And character, to be complete, requires the beautiful and the soft, as well as the imposing; it should have grace in combination with strength; it should display the attractive and the lovely, as well as the sublime. Let it have the devotion inspired by faith, the firmness prescribed by principle, the noble attitude of a high-toned and unimpeachable honour; let it have all this, and we will give it the tribute of our homage, and acknowledge its obvious superiority; but still we want something more—we want something to engage the heart as well as to secure the understanding; something to love as well as to respect; we want the bland and courteous in demeanour; we want 'grace poured into the lips;' we want to lose the awe inspired by the strength of virtue, while listening to the voice and luxuriating in the view of her tenderness. We want, in short, the union of all that is firm in principle, and all that is fervent in piety, and all that is commanding in worth—with whatever is attractive in manners or amiable in feeling; and with all that can sweeten, and soothe, and satisfy, in the contact of ordinary intercourse." *

We claim not for the subject of these pages, superhuman excellencies or angelic perfection. He was a man of like passions with ourselves. No microscopic eye was necessary to discover in him some, though few, of the foibles incident to human life. What we claim for him is:—that he was a man of pure character and noble spirit, a man of high principle and purpose, with a singularly genial nature, a man under the supreme control of Christian truth and love, and who subordinated everything to the call of duty to God and man. In a degree, far above the ordinary standard of Christian attainment, he possessed the *greatness* and *completeness* of character described in the above quotation, and combined in admirable proportions what was unbending in principle and noble in aim, with what was kind in disposition, and saintly in life. His great self-reliance and force of will led him on to success where many men would have failed. Having fixed his aims in life, he was earnest, straightforward, and resolute in pursuing them. Fowell

---

* REV. T. BINNEY.—"The Practical Power of Faith."

Buxton wrote, "The longer I live, the more I am certain that the great difference between men, between the feeble and the powerful, the great and the insignificant, is *energy—invincible determination*—a purpose once fixed, and then death or victory! That quality will do anything that can be done in this world; and no talents, no circumstances, no opportunities, will make a man without it." Mr. Blackburn possessed this quality in a large degree.

An intelligent friend writes respecting him:—

"His character was full of fine and noble qualities. He had a very tender conscience, and a high sense of duty. He was as perfectly ingenuous as any person I ever knew. In him was no guile. He was ever true to his convictions, engagements, and attachments. Although a man of strong emotional power, he was governed by principle, not by feeling. Unselfishness and generosity were specially prominent in him. He lived not for himself, but others. The poor and suffering have often been gladdened by his timely aid; and his friends noted the disinterestedness of his disposition, not only in matters of greater moment, but also—which is a rarer thing—in his thoughtful attentiveness to the smaller courtesies of life. He appeared to be ever thinking how he could prevent the suffering, and promote the welfare of those with whom he had to do. In looking back over the term of my acquaintanceship with him, I cannot recall one single instance in which he ever did a mean or selfish thing. His was a noble soul, and tender as a woman's. He was never so happy as when ministering to the wants of others. Sacrifice was nothing to him where he could do a service."

In abnegation of self, he exceeded most men I have known, and was a conspicuous example of fidelity to principle and conscience. Mercenary motives or social advantage had little power to influence him, when the great concerns of duty or Christian service were involved. His generous impulses proved themselves by practical benevolence, and were fed and intensified by the fruit they produced. He habitually dedicated to God, and distributed to Christian and philanthropic purposes one-fifth of his income; and during his ministry this was by no means large. His entrance on the work of the ministry was not for "the loaves and fishes" to be had, for apparently these commodities were much more readily attainable out of the ministry than in it. The clear voice of God, the commanding call of duty, and great religious earnestness determined his course."

The features of his ministry may be briefly summarised, as they are illustrated by his diary, and by the communications of friends, inserted in these pages.

He was a faithful and earnest preacher. His sermons were scriptural in matter, methodically arranged, always directed to secure the edification of the Church and the conversion of men, and often marked by powerful and affectionate appeal. He was by no means an orator; and was always more anxious about the *thing* to be said than the *manner* of saying it. Sometimes his sermons were almost Puritanic in the number of their divisions and sub-divisions, and occasionally a little halting in his utterance was noticeable; but the aim and earnestness of the preacher were never obscure, and often had they the highest sanction of all—the Spirit sanctifying them to the strengthening and comforting of believers, and the conversion of sinners. Each year, too, was marked by an increase on its predecessor, in the efficiency and power of his pulpit efforts; and it is no small testimony to the regard entertained for his Christian character, and to the acceptability of his ministerial services in the congregations he statedly addressed, that he was cordially invited to remain the fourth and concluding year of his probation in the Circuit in which that probation was begun. This is not an event altogether unique in Methodist Churches; but is of such rare occurrence as to be significant when it does take place.

He was an energetic Evangelist. It has been the glory of the Primitive Methodist community that it has been "missionary" in its origin, character, and history. It sprang into existence as a direct result of successful home-missionary effort; its grandest triumphs have been won by the same agency; and if the power and prosperity of its earlier days are to be maintained, there must still be the same earnest evangelistic effort among the masses of the population. Not often has Primitive Methodism had in its ranks a more zealous agent in this work than our sainted friend. As a local preacher, taking his appointments in the village chapels around his native town embraced more than formally conducting the prescribed services; it included going out into "the highways and hedges," and inviting the people to the house of God, and the Saviour of men. In the ministry, similar methods were employed; and the ordinary appointments of the Sabbath—generally including *three* services—were often supplemented by a fourth, in which the gospel was preached in the open air, and gamblers, sabbath-breakers, and drunkards were invited to "Behold the Lamb of God which taketh away the sin of the world."

He was a diligent and discreet family visitor. In this work, his aim was the spiritual profit of his flock, where members of the church were visited, and the awakening of some religious desire where the visiting was general, or "house to house." It was no part of his work to hear and relate the news of the neighbourhood, or to make his visits occasions of gossip, but rather to stimulate, sympathize with, or counsel, as the circumstances of those he visited might require; and then, in prayer, to commend them to God, and the word of His grace, which is able to build them up, and to give them "an inheritance among all them which are sanctified." A kindly enquiry after the health and welfare of *each* member of the household, a few minutes cheerful conversation on the general interests of the family, temporal and spiritual, an invitation to the service, if such were about to be held, and then a few words of earnest prayer, constituted his method of family visiting. Abundant personal observation enables the writer to certify to the accuracy of this description. With little reservation, he might employ St. Paul's language :—" Ye know from the first day that I came.   after what manner I have been with you in all seasons, serving the Lord with all humility of mind, and with many tears and temptations; and how I kept back nothing that was profitable unto you, but have shewed you, and have taught you publicly, and from house to house, testifying   repentance towards God, and faith toward our Lord Jesus Christ."

And not only was Mr. Blackburn's pastoral work excellent in quality, but abundant in quantity. Connexional rule requires Primitive Methodist ministers, who are superintendents, to visit thirty families each week, and those who are not superintendents, forty families each week, on the average; and when it is remembered how much time is absorbed in superintending the affairs of a circuit on the one hand, and the severe mental application required from probationers on the other, it will be admitted that the standard fixed is by no means a low one; and he who regularly and conscientiously reaches it, merits the appellation of a general family visitor. Mr. Blackburn, however, habitually went beyond it. His diary states, that in 1875, his average number of visits was above forty-six; in 1876 more than forty-five; and in 1877 more than forty-eight. It need scarcely be added that his visits to the sick and poor were warmly welcomed; and when sickness and poverty were found together, it was no unusual thing for him to go and purchase what was requisite for the comfort of the patient, and if no other help was at hand himself *assist* in preparing it.

He took a profound interest in the welfare of young people. This led him to form evening classes, for the mental and moral improvement of the young people of the congregation and Sunday School. In this department he toiled with cheerfulness and success, at one time two evenings each week—Friday and Saturday—being given up solely to this work. In his lessons he had regard to such matters as would permanently benefit his charge; and as the education of many of them had been neglected in their early years, he combined with moral instruction what might be of use to them in the daily occupations of life. There can be no doubt that by working in this hive, he was serving his generation, and answering the great purposes of his ministry. The Church of Christ has no more solemn and pressing problem to solve, than how to win the allegiance of the young to her Master and herself. As a community, we have in the past gained large increases of members *by con-*

quest, by the conversion of adults to Christ; it remains for us to gain similar increases *by growth*, by training our children "in the nurture and admonition of the Lord," and by binding to Christ and to our Connexional ordinances, in living faith, grateful attachment, and loyal service, the hundreds of thousands of young people in our Sunday Schools. To a friend he writes:—" Last Sabbath evening twelve of the Sunday Scholars came to the communion rail, seeking Christ, and most of them appeared to find forgiveness. I take great delight in seeing the children come to Jesus, they seem so simple-hearted and loving. I asked one boy why he had come there. He said, 'To get converted.' I then enquired what he meant by getting converted; and he replied, 'Giving up bad words, lying, stealing, &c.' I thought it would be a blessing if all professing Christians would adopt equally practical views. 'The kingdom of God is not meat and drink, but *righteousness*, and peace, and joy in the Holy Ghost.' Many seem to look upon conversion as a mysterious door into a selfish heaven, without any change of life. 'Not every one that saith unto Me Lord, Lord, shall enter into the kingdom of heaven; but he that *doeth* the will of My Father which is in heaven."

The foregoing pages will have enabled the reader to form a fairly correct idea of missionary work in Fernando Po, and of the adaptability of our departed friend to efficiently perform it. Brief as was his career, it was long enough to indicate what might have been had life and opportunity been prolonged.

He had a true conception of missionary work among a purely heathen population. Primarily, this is religious in its character, but it includes, as essential elements, educational and industrial operations. The missionary must unite to his own spiritual functions, those of the schoolmaster and agriculturalist. Civilization and Christianity must go together, if the heathen are to be permanently blessed. With the Bible in the one hand, the missionary must take the spade, or the axe, or the hammer in the other; and while not neglecting the preaching of the gospel, he must join to it the practice of medicine, and the skill and labour of the artizan. He must be ready to fell trees, and build boats or houses with the timber; he must be prepared to cultivate the soil, that he may teach his charge how to provide for their needs by its rich produce; and he must be willing to turn his hand to any and every form of profitable toil likely to civilise and elevate the people.

Whenever Christianity comes in contact with heathenism, it reveals wants unknown before. The savage roaming the woods builds himself a house; the few roots or fruits that have been his staple food, are supplemented by the crops and harvest of cultivated lands; and the scanty clothing of skins or leaves, are thrown aside for an attire more in harmony with the requirements and decencies of civilised life. In providing for these changes, the missionary must play a prominent part; and Mr. Blackburn was prepared, not only to support, but to initiate all measures of an educational and industrial character, likely to start and stimulate those to whom he was sent, on the path to civilised and Christian life.

He had high qualifications for effective service in this work. His eminently social nature and great kindness of heart attracted the confidence and secured the esteem of the people; his plodding energy enabled him to toil persistently at any task to which he had committed himself; while the absence of conventionalism in his tastes and habits, and his power of adapting himself to almost any circumstances in which he might be placed, qualified him to meet, with ease and promptness, the multifarious duties and opportunities of missionary life among the Bubis of Fernando Po. His unexpected removal from George's Bay to Santa Isabel, speedily followed by the sudden close of life and work, prevented the execution of plans he had formed for the further development of missionary labour. His tact, talents, and devotion gave promise of a missionary career of more than usual energy and success. But his day of active service has closed. His "Sun has gone down while it is yet day."

Section II.—Testimonies to Worth and Service.

"A GOOD name is rather to be chosen than great riches." That our revered friend made this selection, these pages have shown; and that he received, in consequence, a reward that riches cannot give, in the confidence, esteem, and affection of his ministerial fellow-workers, and of those among whom he lived and laboured, the accompanying testimonies to worth and service will show. They are selected from a large number of communications which have been received, and might have been considerably extended. Each contribution is prefaced by the name of its author.

Mr. C. CRABTREE, Circuit Steward at Bingley—

"I became acquainted with the late Rev. R. S. Blackburn on his entering the ministry, when he was appointed to this (Bingley) Circuit. From his first efforts, it was fully apparent that he had special qualifications for the work of the Primitive Methodist ministry. During the three years he remained in this Circuit, he fully sustained the first impressions his character and services made; and though we cannot speak of him as being eloquent in his pulpit efforts, yet his preaching was plain and practical, and marked by much earnestness; his chief aim being to benefit rather than dazzle or please.

"In family visiting, especially among the sick and the aged, he was quite at home; and he took great delight in this department of work. In his social intercourse with the people, he was exceedingly agreeable and pleasant. Having occasion to mingle frequently with the different congregations of the Circuit, I find that in all circles in which he moved he was held in the same high estimation; and in all my associations with our Church, I cannot remember hearing one disparaging word respecting him. In every place his labours were appreciated, and his zeal admired, both by the Church and the general public.

"In this Circuit his name is 'fragrant as ointment poured forth,' and his memory will be fresh and green for many years to come. May the good seed sown by this earnest toiler produce an abundant harvest of blessing to man, and largely promote the glory of God!"

Mr. T. BERRY, a local preacher in the Bingley Circuit—

"My first knowledge of Mr. Blackburn was gained when in July, 1875, he commenced his ministerial life in thi

Circuit. In the same month I was appointed to preach at the Bingley Camp Meeting, and heard him for the first time. His text—a fitting one as the key-note of his ministry—was 'But God forbid that I should glory, save in the cross of our Lord Jesus Christ;' and I shall not soon forget the impression this discourse made on my mind. It was evident that the preacher was thirsting for entire sanctification, which I believe he soon afterwards attained.

"During his ministry here, he was untiring in his efforts to promote the interests of the Church; and he was never afraid of sacrificing his own comfort, time, or treasure, when an opportunity to do good was available. His excellent business training was turned to good purpose in his ministerial work. He was prompt and methodical in all he did. As I review his labours amongst us, it is with genuine pleasure that I remember his diligence in pastoral visiting, his anxiety to influence for good the young, and his zeal for the salvation of souls. These never flagged or abated during the whole of his stay in this Circuit."

Rev. J. AYRTON—

"It affords me pleasure to say that I had the highest opinion of our lamented Brother Blackburn. From repeated occasions of intercourse with him, extending over a period of more than two years, I had opportunities of forming an estimate of his character. I must say that, besides special industriousness in the duties of the ministry, I discovered in him a *noble aim*, and *pureness, lovingness,* and *liberality* in an eminent degree. These were essential qualifications for the hazardous post, the duties of which he so cheerfully undertook.

"I rejoiced on reading of his success in his new sphere,

but in the midst of such rejoicing came the sad news of his departure! His death is a Connexional loss, and it has been felt by me as a personal bereavement. How truly the poet says :—

> 'Somewhere at every hour,
> The watchman on the tower
> Looks forth and sees the fleet
> Approach of the hurrying feet
> Of messengers that bear
> The tidings of despair!'

Our comfort is, that at the resurrection, our Great Master 'will swallow up death in victory.'"

Rev. J. G. LAWRENCE—

" As I had the great pleasure of enjoying the intimate friendship of the Rev. R. S. Blackburn, I got a deep insight into his character. He was possessed of a beautiful nature, whether considered in a social or moral aspect. He inherited both a strong passion for society, and, in an eminent degree, those social qualities which make a person's society valued and sought after. However, he was perfectly accessible only to certain natures; in his judgment, friendship was too sacred to be common. His private thoughts and feelings were, so to speak, apartments which only a select few were allowed to enter; books which they only had the privilege of reading.

" Between the moral tendencies of his nature there was equilibrium. Strong feeling was checked by strict conscientiousness and good sense, and judgment of human failings was softened by benevolent dispositions. He had no sympathy with what was mean. His love of truth an right was so strong that he did not spare reproof even to friends, when it was called for.

"To our dear friend, God was not a cold, lifeless abstraction—He was a living, personal Being, filling the heart and life with His presence. Religion was not creed or ceremony, or both; it was principle, experience, and character. Christian morality was not the expediency of moral actions —it was the harmony of all the soul's thoughts and affections with the Divine will. And these holy truths he daily felt and lived. He was a man of prayer. He strove after Christian advancement, and longed for the sinless life of which St. John speaks, and which was often the subject of conversation between us.

"As a Christian worker, he was intensely earnest, and in labours abundant. His aim was not to preach great sermons, but to win souls to the Saviour. He was a faithful friend, a real Christian, and an earnest toiler in the Lord's vineyard. Little did I think that he would so soon finish his work on earth. How mysterious are the ways of Providence! The fact that his death can be explained by natural causes, does not set aside the doctrine of a permissive Providence. Many men are permitted to outlive their usefulness; but God called him to lay down his life in the flower of his age, and the vigour of early manhood. He often told me that should he enter the ministry, he would go abroad, if practicable. His heart's desire was granted, but at the expense of life itself."

Rev. H. CRABTREE—

"From the time Mr. Blackburn became a member of the Primitive Methodist Connexion to the time of his departure for Liverpool, *en-route* for Fernando Po, I had ample opportunities of becoming acquainted with many of the phases of his moral and religious character. In all my observations, I never discovered anything like cant, or affectation, or reserve; he was natural, sincere, open, affable, and easy of access; remarkable for self-abnegation, and signally free from self-inflated airs or clerical starch.

"Religion, in his case, was not a sombre thing; he did not seek his happiness in meditation among the tombs, or in the intonation of funeral dirges. It was emphatically 'Joy in the Holy Ghost.' He was in his element when singing—

> 'Then let our songs abound,
>   And every tear be dry;
> We're marching through Emmanuel's ground,
>   To fairer worlds on high.'

"There was nothing boisterous or vociferous in his manner; no distorted features, no muscular contortions. He was calm, deliberate, and impressive. Had he lived a few years longer, I do not suppose that he would have become a pulpit star of the first magnitude, amazing people by depth or brilliancy of thought, or by rhetorical flourishes; but I am sure he would have been a very acceptable and successful pastor and missionary, and a creditable preacher.

"When taking leave of me in the Station, Leeds, he cheerfully said, 'If I have my health and am useful, I intend to stay some years in Africa. Farewell!'

> 'We shall meet beyond the river,
>   Where the surges never roll.'"

"Rev. C. Rumfitt—

"I am at a loss what to say respecting the death of our late dear Bro. Blackburn; so impressed am I with the inscrutability of God's ways in this matter, that I can only conclude that we must class it with those things the meaning of which we cannot know until the great hereafter. That he should be called to relinquish a profitable and useful career as a 'layman,' for only three years of ministerial toil; that his going to Africa should be contingent on another brother's illness; and that while there, he should be cut off at a time when he himself was preparing in high expectation for marriage; and also when the church in Africa required his life rather than his death, are features of the event which we cannot understand, and must leave, consoled only by the fact, that it is the Master's doing, and therefore must be right.

"I am exceedingly happy to have an opportunity of bearing my testimony to Bro. Blackburn's worth; during his ministerial life, I have occasionally met with him in private and public, and have been much impressed by his excellencies.

"I ever considered that he was manly, and thoroughly *genuine*, with not the least shade of sham or pretence. No one could be much in his company without seeing that his piety was solid, which in these days of hollowness and varnish is a great desideratum.

"As a minister, I should place him among the *useful* rather than the *brilliant*; most useful and esteemed where met with the oftenest, viz., where he resided. I should think his sermons, as a rule, would be eminently practical. But judging from his disposition, I should say that his great 'forte' was visiting the homes of his people, in which he would be particularly useful in bringing men to Jesus Christ, and had his life been spared very many souls would have been the crown of his rejoicing.

"We can ill afford to part with him, but it is God's doing, and we must submit.

"I pray that his friends may be divinely comforted, and that his death may teach important lessons to us all."

"Rev. S. B. REYNOLDS—

"During my last term of four years' ministry in the Pontefract Circuit, I had ample opportunities of forming an estimate of the character of our late lamented friend and brother, Richard Stead Blackburn. During that period, he was raised to the position of an accredited local preacher on the Circuit plan; he also studied for, underwent, and successfully passed, the usual examinations preparatory to entering our regular ministry.

"I entertained, then, the highest regard for him as a man, a friend, and Christian; and I have only been more confirmed in my opinion since. I always found him ready to do anything in his power to lessen human woe, or promote the happiness of his fellow-creatures, advance the kingdom of Christ generally, and the cause of Primitive Methodism in particular. He took a deep interest in the new chapel movements in the Circuit, especially the town chapel, and in many ways contributed liberally to aid its funds. He also became a trustee for other chapels in the station, and thought nothing too much that he could do to carry on successful the work of God, upon which his heart was fixed. F threw his heart and soul into the " Good Templar " mov ment, even in the face of the great trade interests in tl place, and at the risk of much loss in their own business. He had only to be convinced that a thing was right, and then fearless of all consequences, he would throw himself into it.

"He was a generous giver. He adopted, and scrupulously practised the principle of systematic giving. The poor and the afflicted were the objects of his special attention and help.

"He was a lover of the means of grace, and was regular in his attendance at the preaching services, and the class meeting, when not unavoidably prevented. He never thought he was above the necessity of having his *own* soul fed and watered. He was beloved and esteemed by all, but most by those who knew him best. I knew him intimately, prized him highly, and loved him dearly as a friend and a brother.

"He was 'not slothful in business, but fervent in spirit, serving the Lord.' He made a great temporal sacrifice on entering the ministry among us; but he carefully counted the cost, and was fully prepared for it.

"As a man, he was upright and conscientious; as a friend, affectionate and faithful; as a Christian, devout and sincere; as a minister, zealous and enthusiastic; and I fear he has fallen a victim to over-working. Many may have had a more brilliant, but none a more sincere or well-meant career than his.

"'The memory of the just is blessed;' and 'the righteous shall be in everlasting remembrance.'"

"Rev. T NEWELL, President of the Conference—

"I think it will be difficult for Primitive Methodists to place too high an estimate on the personal worth of the late Mr. Blackburn, and upon the services he has rendered, short as his career has been, to the Church of his choice and love. We may not speak of him as a man of brilliant parts, or of great intellectual promise. Had he lived, it is probable he would not have attained to literary distinction, to eminence as a theologian, or to remarkable pulpit power; so that we cannot set him up as a pattern, in these respects, for our young men to follow. His talents and tastes led in another direction, and his excellencies were of a different kind; and yet they were of a kind quite as necessary to the carrying on of the Lord's work, as any stores of erudition, or charms of oratory for which the church of Jesus has been noted in its past life.

" It is likely that our brother would have always wielded greater power out of the pulpit than in it, however long his ministerial life had been. He had more influence with men to unlock their hearts, than to open their understandings, or to get hold of their consciences. By his geniality of spirit, his frank and cheerful disposition, his kindness to the poor, his generosity, his noble self-sacrifice, and his readiness for any kind of work that would build up the Master's cause, he won upon all he had to do with; and no doubt, if God had seen fit to give him length of days, he would have done much more than many men, greatly his superiors in intellectual grasp, to make manifest the beauty and fragrance of a truly Christian character and life.

" His removal from our midst is certainly one of the mournful and mysterious chapters in the history of our Church. But the event is not altogether melancholy; there are bright spots, not a few, in this painful and perplexing bereavement. Already it is bearing fruit for good. Evidently our brother's fall has deepened the interest which

Primitive Methodists feel in the work to which he gave himself. I have been no little impressed with the fact that, notwithstanding the perilous nature of this African mission work, and while Brother Blackburn's ashes are yet warm, as we may say, no fewer than three of his brethren have expressed their readiness to take up the sword which he can no longer use, and to do battle against the enemy in the high places of the field. Perhaps it was needful, in order that the missionary fire might be preserved and intensified among us, for someone to dare, and do, and die, as our brother did. I am not sure that our zeal for Africa had not begun to cool. Let us hope that the death of this brave young man will greatly fan the flame. Henceforth we shall be bound to this mission as we were never bound before. Although we shall see our brother's face no more in the flesh, and are greatly afflicted by his sudden removal from the post of duty, both ministers and people will bless God for a life as bright as it was brief, and will listen, again and again, with mingled sadness and pleasure, to the voice that is borne to us on the breezes from the fever swamps of Fernando Po; and that speaks to us in words more eloquent and soul-stirring than any living lips can utter, of disinterestedness, patient endurance, fortitude, self-denial, and heroic devotion to the cause of Christ and humanity. While our religion continues to kindle such enthusiasm, and form such noble characters as we have in our departed friend, we need never fear for its safety and progress. I pray that our loss may greatly help in the work of saving Africa.

"Rev. T BARRON—

"In August, 1878, he sailed for Fernando Po, where,

after eight months' labours, he laid down his weary head to die in calm assurance of eternal life. He counted not his life dear unto himself, so that he might finish his course with joy, and the ministry which he had received of the Lord Jesus, to testify of the Gospel of the grace of God. How soon and unexpectedly that course and ministry were finished! How brief, and yet how bright, was his career on earth! We watched him tread the upward path with brotherly pride and love; we rejoiced in his success as he won the favour of the people among whom he dwelt, and added stone to stone in the temple of redeemed humanity; we augured for him many years of honoured toil in the Master's vineyard. Our hearts followed him to Western Africa, and joyfully anticipated the time when, his missionary laurels won, we should give him a loving welcome to his native land. We received, from time to time, communications telling of his varied and heavy work, and uninterrupted health and happiness. In a letter dated April 12th, ten days before he died, we rejoiced to read that, in spite of double work and intense heat, he was as well as when he left England, and was busily preparing to receive his bride. He was bright with hope; and now, he has gone. It was in his heart to build a noble house of personal godliness and relative usefulness unto the Name of the Lord. He was permitted to lay a good foundation, and build enough to show his compeers that the structure, when completed, would stand out radiant with the smile of God, and would pass unscathed through the searching fires of judgment. He did well that it was in his heart; nevertheless, he was not allowed to build the house. But has the erection come to an eternal stand-still? Has this unfulfilled life found its climax in eternal unconsciousness or annihilation? The Christian revelation of immortality answers with a loud, and joyous, and emphatic, no! The building is yet going on, and going on where no sword of defence is needed. The life, unfulfilled on earth, is transplanted to the more congenial soil of Paradise, and unhampered by defective physical conditions, is pressing forward to the grand consummation of the Great Day of the Lord. Our brother is not dead, he has just begun to live; he has only changed the mode of his being. The Christian cannot die, he never sees death. This noble Christian man and missionary has gone beyond the range of our physical consciousness into the realm of perfected spirits; but our soul-consciousness still holds him in bonds of loving memory and communion, which the ages of the illimitable future will only tighten and strengthen.

"He was no common man. He was not content to tread the easy and ignoble path of Christian mediocrity, but yearned and struggled after the Alpine heights of heroic spiritual life and work. His religion was not a cold, arithmetical balancing of the question, 'What must I do to be safe?' but was an enthusiastic self-abandonment of himself to the will of God, and the good of man. I never knew a man who more throughly incorporated into his moral being the spirit of the grand Pauline utterances, 'To me to live is Christ;' 'This one thing I do.' Christian consecration and concentration were the centre from which radiated, and around which revolved, his beautiful character, and his Christly life. Love to his Lord and Master was the dominant passion of his soul, the all-controlling power of his activities. This supreme divine affection, ruling as a king within him, gave force to his character, beauty to his disposition, joy and peace to his soul, power to his life, and glory to his death. If the sacrifice of self for the highest good of others be the index of true heroism, Richard Stead Blackburn was a hero.

"To know him was to love him dearly, and esteem him highly. From a full heart, I fling these fragments of the high estimate which I have formed of the noble character and career of my tried and trusty, and now sainted friend. I cannot realise that I shall see his face no more. I will not think of him as dead.

> ' Forgive my grief for one removed,
>   Thy creature, whom I found so fair,
>   I trust he lives in Thee, and there
> I find him worthier to be loved.
>
> But who shall so forecast the years,
>   And find in loss a gain to match?
>   Or reach a hand through time to catch
> The far-off interest of tears?
>
> Let love clasp grief lest both be drown'd,
>   Let darkness keep her raven gloss;
>   Ah, sweeter to be drunk with loss,
> To dance with death, to beat the ground,
>
> Than that the victor hours should scorn
>   The long result of love, and boast,
>   "Behold the man that loved and lost,
> But all he was is overworn."
>
> Thrice blest whose lives are faithful prayers,
>   Whose loves in higher love endure;
>   What souls possess themselves so pure,
> Or is there blessedness like their's.'
>
> "IN MEMORIAM."

Rev. W. B. LUDDINGTON, now of Fernando Po, successor to Mr. Blackburn at the George's Bay Station—.

"Though sitting in the room where our devoted Brother Blackburn breathed his last, I can hardly realize the fact that, in the flesh, we shall see his face no more. As I write these lines, the circumstances connected with this mission during the last eighteen months, some of them perplexing and painful, come vividly before my mind.

"It is not unlikely, on constitutional grounds, that Mr. Blackburn might ultimately have become a victim to the climate; yet occurring *when* and *as* it did, his death can be regarded as little short of a martyrdom. It is easy to be wise after the event, and whether it would not have been better to have made the voyages less frequently, and to have stayed a little longer each time at the Bay, we need not discuss now. Mr. Blackburn believed the course he took was necessary, and believing this, he shrunk from nothing that the work required.

"What that work involves in this climate, and on this island, none but those who have had personal experience of it can thoroughly understand. Long boat journeys, with the burning rays of a tropical sun directly overhead, followed by the heavy dews of the night, or overtaken, or met by a sweeping tornado, and drenched and soaked with the pelting rain, together with the debilitating effect of the climate, the care of the churches so far apart, and the absence of the companionship and counsel another European Missionary would have furnished, made the conditions of his work here peculiarly trying.

"Each one of his predecessors on this island has suffered much, but he has been the first to fall. Doubtless, the Allwise Father will make the mysterious event minister to some grand purpose. Sad and sorrowful must have been the feelings of the little Christian band on the evening when their missionary lay cold in death. All through the livelong night they, so recently rescued from heathenism through the instrumentality of the mission, testified to their love and sorrow for their departed pastor, by watching over his remains, waiting for the morning light, and mourning for the loss they had sustained.

" By his affable and cheerful manners, and visitation from house to house, Mr. Blackburn made friends amongst both black and white residents in Isabel, and will be long remembered. In his early death the Connexion has *lost* an earnest worker, and a heroic Missionary of the Cross. What it has *gained* the future may show. Surely other young men will imbibe his brave and Apostolic spirit, and will see to it that our West African Missions never droop for want of workers. Fernando Po has become all the dearer to us, as Primitive Methodists, because one of our most laborious young ministers has found in its soil an early grave. His coffined form lying in the Fernandian bush, forbids the thought that there should ever be any decline of sympathy with, or support of, the missions on this island. The remembrance of his readiness to do, or die, as the Master saw best, will surely act as a powerful stimulus through all the future, when the spiritual enlightenment and moral renovation of these heathen Bubis are the subject of consideration. I pray that we may have the joy of meeting our brother again in the land where the wild tornado never blows, where the fever never rages, and where the inhabitants need no candle, neither light of the sun, for the Lord God giveth them light, and they shall reign for ever and ever."

Section III.—Letters of Condolence.

A FEW selections from a large number of communications expressive of deep sympathy with Mr. Blackburn's relatives and friends in their sad and sudden bereavement, may not unfittingly be inserted here. They form a chaplet of evergreens with which to crown the memory of our now sainted friend; soothing the sorrows of others than those to whom they originally came, who scan these lines and in times of bereavement and affliction :—

"Primitive Methodist Missions.
"*Deputy Treasurer's Office,*
"*London, S.W.*"

"Mr. Blackburn, Pontefract.
"My dear Sir,
"I have just learned that the Primitive Methodist Conference at Leeds appointed me to express the feelings of profound sympathy with you and your family which that assembly cherished when they heard of the death of your devoted son—the Rev. R. S. Blackburn, of Fernando Po. The death of such a Missionary was a great loss to the Church of Christ, and to the heathen world, and must have been especially painful to you. This loss has happened under the direction of a Father who loves his human children more than they can love each other; but He sees and knows what they cannot. Assured that the Almighty cannot err, and that His loving-kindness fails not, we can only bow and wait : the mystery of His Providence will be revealed hereafter. Meanwhile you have the assurance that your departed son was accepted of the Saviour, that his life was nobly consecrated, and was laid down in the service of the

Redeemer and humanity. He lived, laboured, and died in sympathy with Him 'Who gave Himself for us.' He has finished his work—the recompense of reward has been vouchsafed. He overcame, and is seated with the Saviour. May Divine grace be given to his bereaved family, so that they may follow him as he followed Christ!

"I am, dear Sir,
"Yours affectionately,
"S. ANTLIFF."

"17, *Princes Garden*,
"*9th June*, 1879.

"Dear Mr. Blackburn,

"Pray accept my most sincere condolence, on the death of your son, at Santa Isabel. When you asked me to write to the Foreign Office about the Mission there, I little thought that the next I was to hear about him, would be of so melancholy a nature. It must be some sad satisfaction to you to know that he was so much respected and beloved.

"Believe me to be,
"Yours very truly,
"HUGH C. E. CHILDERS."

Soon after Mr. Blackburn left England, the Ministerial Association of the Leeds district passed the following resolution, and directed its secretary, Rev. T. Markwell, to forward it to Fernando Po:—

"That we congratulate the Rev. R. S. Blackburn on his appointment to the glorious work of a Missionary to the heathen in Fernando Po; that we express to him our hearty sympathy and good wishes, and assure him of our prayers that his health may be preserved, and his services in that distant land made signally successful."

On learning the painful fact of his sudden death, the same assembly of ministers sent to the bereaved parent the annexed tribute :—

"That we record our deep sense of the great loss the connexion at large, and this district in particular, have sustained by the early decease of the Rev. R. S. Blackburn, whilst zealously engaged in Foreign Missionary work in the Island of Fernando Po."

From a Christian Worker—

"With deep regret I learn to-day the death of the brave young missionary, to whom a year ago I sent the leaflet, 'Good bye, or 'God be with you.' Here are some lines on

BUT FOR A MOMENT.

"Only a little 'moment,'
  Treading where he has trod,
And the earnest weary toiler
  Stands face to face with God.

"Only a little 'moment.'
  No need to say 'Good bye,
No time to shed a parting tear,
  The meeting is so nigh."

"*Wilsden, June* 2, 1879.

"MY DEAR ——

"I am deeply pained by the sad intelligence which has just reached me of the comparatively sudden death of our old and valued friend, Mr. Blackburn, and deeply sympathise with you and with your Missionary Society under the loss you have sustained, and with you particularly in the sorrow which, I am sure, you must and do feel in consequence of this lamentable event. But all things are in the

Great Master's hands, and He has done it, mysterious as it appears to us. I think it was Luther who used to say that 'God's Ministers were immortal till their work was done;' and now we must conclude that our brother's work was done. To us it seemed but just begun, but He who said 'Go work,' has thought otherwise, and has put an end to the labour, apparently while it was noon-day. Perhaps it was that the Lord of the vineyard accounted our brother's cheerful entrance upon a part of that vineyard, where there are so many discomforts and so many risks, and his short period of earnest work there, as equal to a long life's work elsewhere, and so took him to a full and much earlier reward. At all events the Lord knows best, and He has given to His servant the honour of falling in the field, and He will comfort those who most mourn the very bitter bereavement.

"I am yours, very sincerely,
"JAMES BULLOCK."

" 16, *Beckett-street, Leeds, June* 23*rd*, 1879.
"DEAR SISTER IN THE LORD,

"I am instructed by the quarterly meeting of the officials of the Leeds 1st Circuit to write you expressing the deep sorrow they feel for you in the sad bereavement you have now to experience. We pray that you may be divinely sustained under this afflictive dispensation, and led to believe that your Heavenly Father will lay no more upon you than you are able to bear. The loss of Bro. Blackburn is an irreparable one, so far as earth or this life is concerned, but in heaven, where he now is, there will be a re-union of kindred spirits, and the bond shall never more be severed. May the God of all grace comfort you with the consolations of His Word. Be resigned to His will, and all things will work together for your good. I can assure you that you have the deep sympathies of all the Circuit. May you have God's strength to enable you to bear this trial patiently for Jesus' sake.

"With kind regards, yours faithfully, and in sorrow,

"W H. KERSHAW"

" Miss Crabtree."

"*Bedford, June 8th,* 1879.

" My dear, dear Friend,

"God comfort thee ! God comfort thee ! Oh, my darling child, how I do feel for you ! Fain would I soothe you on my bosom as a mother comforts her child, whispering soft gentle words of healing support and strength. Oh, how thankful I feel that you know well where to seek for help in this most trying hour. I feel persuaded that, although the way appears so dark, and God's Providence so mysterious, you will still trust in Him who is 'too wise to err, too good to be unkind.' My precious friend, I almost tremble to meddle with such grief as yours. Oh, what a change has come over the spirit of my dream concerning you since last Sunday ! It has, indeed, been a sad time to me since we received the dreadful news ; but I shudder to think what it must have been to you. Our prayers have been incessant that you might have strength given to you according to your great need. I felt that your Heavenly Father would sustain you and bring you back to the wide open arms and loving, sympathetic, but aching hearts, so longing to receive you. Upon you has the trouble fallen, my dear girl, not upon your truest friend. Knowing your nature, I know you would rather have it so than the reverse. *It is well with him,* be assured ; and although his sun has set whilst it was yet high day, he had finished the work his Master had given him to do, and he now enjoys his reward. Brave soul! he has joined the martyr throng! Fear not, you shall go to him, although he may not return to you. He may be permitted to be, yea, doubtless is, another 'angel guide' to you, although, like Mrs. Judson, you may say—

> 'Down life's dim labyrinth
>   I grope my way alone,
> While wildly through the midnight sky
>   Black hurrying clouds are blown,
> And thickly in my tangled path
>   The sharp bare thorns are sown.
> Yet firm my foot, for well I know
>   The goal cannot be far,
> And ever, through the rifted clouds,
>   Shines out one steady star:
> For when my guide went up, he left
>   The pearly gates ajar.'

And now I commend you to God. My head aches much, for my tears will flow.

"Ever with you in spirit, yours in deepest sympathy and warmest love,

" AMELIA.

"P.S.—I feel as if I had said nothing I would say, but my heart has seemed too full for words."

"*Burton-on-Trent.*

"MY DEAR FRIEND,

"At last I may write to you; and now what can I say? Words fail me to express the deep sympathy which I feel for you in this crowning trial of all the rest, the heaviest, the severest! Dear, dear friend, would that I could help you, could by word or act give you the least grain of comfort.

"My first knowledge of the great trouble which had come into your life was almost accidental. My grief was intense; my heart-ache for you such as I never before experienced. It seemed *too* hard for you, too sad to be true; and gradually taking in all the sad position in which you were placed, my heart was too full of grief to be able to do anything but pray, beseech, agonize for you to the Great Comforter, imploring Him to hold you in His strong, loving arms, while the storm of grief swept over you.

"Feeling that our sympathy, though very great for you, would not be able to reach you, to touch you in this sorrow, I did not write sooner; I felt that words were no expression of what I felt.

"I have no grief for the joy, the triumph, the exultation, the reward which the devoted martyr-spirit now enjoys. Great must be the reward, glorious his crown of rejoicing. It is impossible to sorrow for the labour ended, the end gained, but the loneliness for you, the cross which you will have to struggle under, and to bear until life's end, is the grief to us. The joy even in this is, that life here *cannot* be very long; the years may weary, but they cannot stay themselves; they cannot delay the time of the re-union in heaven. *That will come*, certainly; nothing can hinder it; and God's loving care round you meanwhile, His great, tender heart pulsating in sympathy with yours, His words saying to the tempests of grief (which do and will come) 'Peace, be still!' shall, as of old, quell the storm, and carry you through; not without pain, not without the marks of the conflict passed through, but 'perfect through suffering, into the land where the meeting will be beyond all that our finite minds can conceive of infinite joy.

"We are all awed by the mysterious Providence which has taken the young, strong, zealous spirit to Himself, leaving a great gap in the work, which apparently he was so well able to fill. And now we can only wait and trust for the meaning, the purpose of this which lies hidden, and some day it will come out clear as the day.

"I will close now.
"With dearest love, and most heart-felt sympathy,
"I remain,
"Yours affectionately,
"ANNIE."

"*Mission Besé, George's Bay.*
"*Nov. 28th*, 1879.

"He was greatly beloved by every one here, both black and white; oh! how greatly we miss him. May He who has gone before prepare a place for us in the final meeting.
"Yours affectionately,
"M. PETERS."

Our task is well-nigh done. We leave the reader to gather up for himself the lessons that are powerfully enforced by the manly character and devoted career we have sketched. We have been solicitous, solely, to present a faithful picture of the subject of these pages, and to furnish a memorial worthy of the noble life he lived. Biography, to be useful, must be faithful and true; and we have aimed to give this Memoir these features. Our departed brother, though not possessed of brilliant parts, was a **genuine**

Christian and a true missionary ; and not the least legacy he has left, is a memory fragrant of what is self-sacrificing and Christ-like.

" If to seek not our own 'profit, but the profit of many that they may be saved,' and to set aside promising prospects of worldly gain to preach the ' unsearchable riches of Christ,' be truly apostolic ;—if the Missionary evinces a spirit noble and heroic, who leaves his native shores, and dwells in a distant land, and in an inhospitable climate, simply to tell 'the story of the Cross' to heathens and savages, that he may enlighten and save, civilise and ennoble them, and, it may be, after a brief period of toil, fall a martyr to the fervour of his zeal, and the devotedness of his work ;—if to be occupied by one mighty thought—the glory of God in the salvation of men, and controlled by one dominant emotion—the constraining love of Christ, be to secure invariably the smile and recognition of God, then among the Apostles, Prophets, and we may add, Martyrs, Kings, and Priests of God, our beloved brother must be assigned a place. He looked not 'on his own things,' 'but on the things of others.' He sought not his own welfare, but the welfare of others He laid body, soul, and spirit on the altar of consecrated service."*

When discoursing to the Ephesian Elders at Miletus, St. Paul desired to " finish his course with joy," and he anticipated the termination of life and work with exultant hope. Then the struggle would be over, the danger past, and the crown of glory won.

---

* Heroism in Missionary Service.

"What a contrast between the day of struggle and the day of victory! Here, the din, dust, and tumult of battle; there, the calm repose of well-won and unquestioned triumph. Here, toil, danger, persecution, bonds, imprisonments, death; there, rest, safety, reward, the 'crown that fadeth not away,' the strains of jubilant song, the welcome and presence of God. Here, ignominy, insult, poverty; there, honours that never pale, pleasures that never end, a service congenial, delightful, everlasting. How welcome the prospect! 'Henceforth there is laid up for me a crown of righteousness, which the Lord, the righteous Judge, shall give me at that day: and not to me only, but unto all them also that love His appearing.'

"Such will still be the triumphant close of every true missionary's life: he shall 'finish his course with joy.' Many things may contribute to the joy of a faithful minister in his closing hour. He has joy arising from personal acceptance with God; his own sin has, through divine mercy, been forgiven; his own heart and life have been purified by divine grace; and 'washed in the blood of the Lamb,' he will enter 'through the gates' into the City. He has joy because, though he die, his works will live. His active presence is withdrawn, but his memory yet lives to influence and ennoble. His name is fragrant 'as ointment poured forth.' 'The memory of the just is blessed.' The labours of the husbandman have ceased; but the seed is there—hid in the soil of human hearts—buried, perhaps forgotten, but vital still, and only waiting for the genial sunshine and shower, to make it burst forth into life and fruitfulness; and the harvest of that sowing shall be reaped long after the sower has entered into rest. And there is joy in the prospect of the immediate and ample reward which all faithful labour will assuredly secure. 'They that be wise shall shine as the brightness of the firmament, and they that turn many to righteousness, as the stars for ever and ever.'

"Such a hope animated the breast of our beloved friend. His ministry closed early—and closed not in darkness and failure, but in light and success. Short as it was, it was long enough to reveal its worth and faithfulness; and to indicate what it might have been had life been spared. 'He sleeps in Jesus.' 'He rests from his labours, and his works follow him.' 'He being dead yet speaketh;' and, in words more eloquent than any that living lips can utter, exclaims, 'Work while it is day, for the night cometh when no man can work.'"

"We check complaining with the thought—God is over all. Our brother's removal can be no incident in the chapter of accidents. Is it not part of God's great plan for the regeneration of Africa? Brief and fragmentary as his life seems, who shall say it is not harmonious and complete? And now God has raised it to the higher and nobler life of heaven. If his death shall deepen our convictions of duty to the Bubis of Fernando Po—if other hands shall spring forward to seize and bear aloft the standard that has fallen from his nerveless grasp—and if the remembrance of his devoted labours shall intensify the zeal and activity of the church with which he was identified, then as he lived not, neither will he have died, in vain."*

---

* Heroism in Missionary Service.

PRINTED BY BEMROSE AND SONS, 10, PATERNOSTER
BUILDINGS, LONDON; AND DERBY.

www.ingramcontent.com/pod-product-compliance
Lightning Source LLC
Chambersburg PA
CBHW020832230426
43666CB00007B/1189